Yuval Noah Harari

Unstoppable Us

― VOLUME 3 ―

Yuval Noah Harari
Unstoppable Us

VOLUME 3

How Enemies Become Friends

Illustrated by **Ricard Zaplana Ruiz**

PUFFIN

PUFFIN BOOKS

UK | USA | Canada | Ireland | Australia
India | New Zealand | South Africa

Puffin Books is part of the Penguin Random House group of companies
whose addresses can be found at global.penguinrandomhouse.com.

www.penguin.co.uk
www.puffin.co.uk
www.ladybird.co.uk

Simultaneously published in the USA by Bright Matter Books,
an imprint of Random House Children's Books,
a division of Penguin Random House LLC, New York,
and in the UK by Puffin Books 2026

001

Text copyright © Yuval Noah Harari, 2026
Cover art and interior illustrations © Sapienship, 2026

The moral right of the author and illustrators has been asserted

C.H.Beck & dtv:
Editors: Susanne Stark, Sebastian Ullrich

Sapienship Storytelling:
Production and management: Itzik Yahav
Management and editing: Naama Avital
Marketing and PR: Naama Wartenburg
Editing and project management: Ariel Retik
Research assistants: Jason Parry, Jim Clarke, Ray Brandon, Dor Shilton
Copy-editing: Adriana Hunter
Design: Hanna Shapiro
Diversity consulting: Adi Moreno

sapienship.co

No part of this book may be used or reproduced in any manner for the purpose of training artificial
intelligence technologies or systems. In accordance with Article 4(3) of the DSM Directive 2019/790,
Penguin Random House expressly reserves this work from the text and data mining exception.

Printed and bound in China

The authorized representative in the EEA is Penguin Random House Ireland,
Morrison Chambers, 32 Nassau Street, Dublin D02 YH68

A CIP catalogue record for this book is available from the British Library

HARDBACK ISBN: 978-0-241-76697-2

INTERNATIONAL PAPERBACK ISBN: 978-0-241-76698-9

All correspondence to:
Puffin Books
Penguin Random House Children's
One Embassy Gardens, 8 Viaduct Gardens, London SW11 7BW

Penguin Random House is committed to a
sustainable future for our business, our readers
and our planet. This book is made from Forest
Stewardship Council® certified paper.

To all beings—those gone, those living, and those still to come. Our ancestors made the world what it is. We can decide what the world will become.

CONTENTS

TIMELINE OF HISTORY xii

A NOTE FROM THE AUTHOR xv

WHAT DO YOU CALL GOD? xvii

ARE YOU LIKE EVERYBODY ELSE? xviii

1: Dragon-People, Ant-People, and Wolf-People 3

2: The Secret of the Market 31

3: The Children of the Bad Guys 65

4: The Meaning of Life 121

WORLD MAP OF HISTORY 176

ACKNOWLEDGMENTS 179

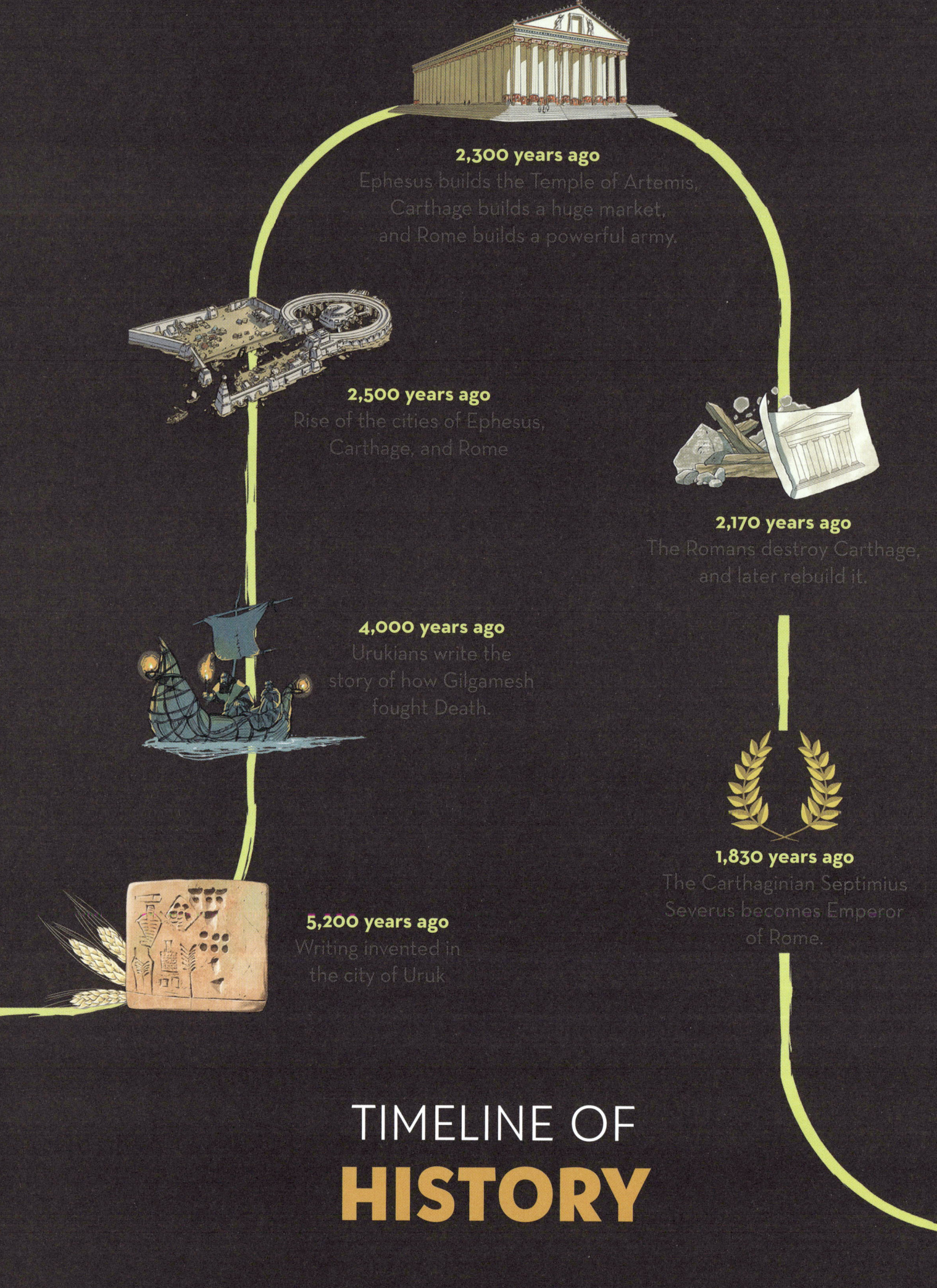

1,570 years ago
The Vandals vandalize Rome.

1,630 years ago
Christians in Carthage decide which stories to put in the Bible, and Christians in Ephesus destroy the Temple of Artemis.

1,325 years ago
The Muslims destroy Carthage.

1,650 years ago
The Romans become Christians.

770 years ago
The Mongol Khan wants to know which story everyone should believe.

1,810 years ago
The people of Carthage and Ephesus become Romans.

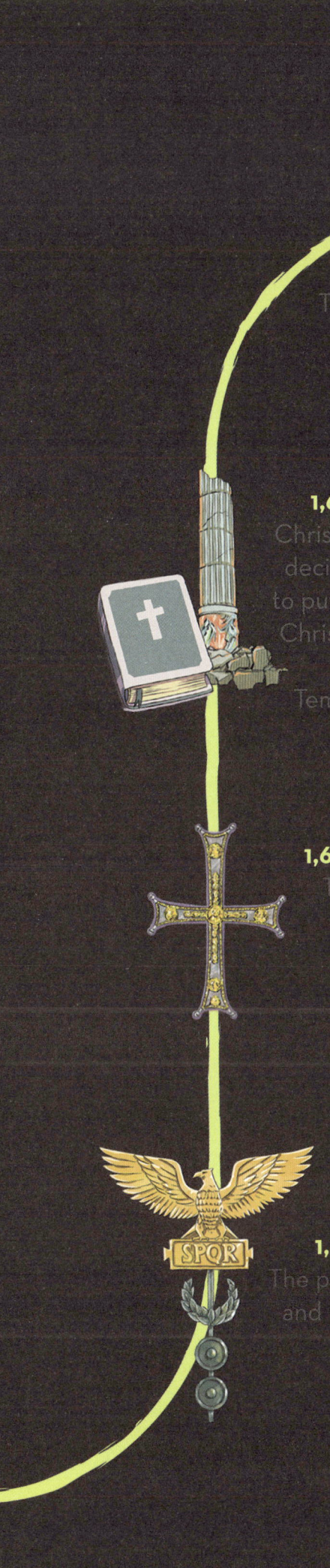

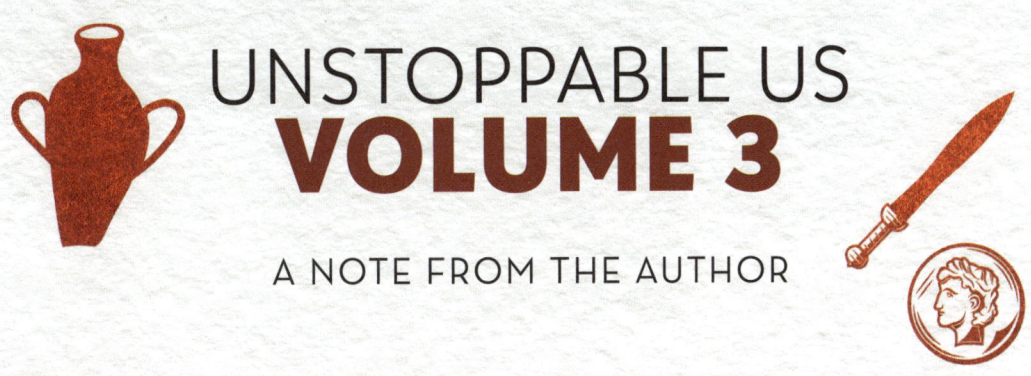

UNSTOPPABLE US
VOLUME 3

A NOTE FROM THE AUTHOR

The events depicted in this book are real events, the places are real places, and historical figures like the Carthaginian general Hanniba'al and the Roman emperor Varius are real figures. However, to enliven the story I have taken the liberty of inventing some fictional characters like the Carthaginian girl Saponiba'al and the Roman sailor Gaius. Every care has been taken to depict events as they could have happened and to illustrate them as they would have looked. To know what took place thousands of years ago, we rely on the stories and objects ancient people left to us. But over thousands of years stories get garbled and objects get lost. So there are many things we do not know about ancient events. I occasionally made educated guesses to fill these gaps.

WHAT DO YOU CALL GOD?

IN THIS BOOK, I CALL THE JEWISH, CHRISTIAN, AND MUSLIM GOD "the Sky Father," and not simply "God." You may wonder why I chose to do that. The reason is that ancient people believed in many different gods, like Zeus and Ba'al, and today too there are people who believe in other gods, like Shiva. And everyone calls their god "God." I wanted to find a term that would differentiate the Jewish, Christian, and Muslim god from all the other gods, even though they share a lot of similarities. I decided to use the term "the Sky Father" because the Jews, Christians, and Muslims all believe their god is like a great father who lives up in the sky.

ARE YOU LIKE
EVERYBODY ELSE?

Do you sometimes feel different from other people? Do you sometimes feel you want to behave differently and think differently than everyone around you, wearing clothes that nobody around you wears, listening to music that nobody else seems to like, or thinking that something is good when everyone else insists it isn't? **Do you sometimes feel people around you want to put you in a box and force you to be someone you don't want to be?**

Some people say being different is bad, because if you think and behave differently than everyone around you, you can't cooperate with them or be friends with them, and they're likely to fight and hurt you. So people who dislike being different say it's best to divide all the world into neat boxes, and make sure every box contains only people who think and behave the same. They have a word for the most important of these neat boxes: They call them "countries," like Greece, Nigeria, India, and Canada. And they call people who aren't from their particular box "foreigners."

These people who like putting everyone in boxes claim that you belong in only one of these countries, and you shouldn't be different from the other people in it. You must speak the same language as everyone, wear the same clothes, listen to the same music, eat the same food, play the same games, and believe in the same gods. If you're different from the other people in your country, you won't get along with them, and it will only cause fights. And if you go to another country, you'll be a foreigner and the people there won't like you, because you don't belong there.

The box-people say this is just how the world is. There were always Greeks who lived in Greece, spoke the Greek language, ate Greek food, played Greek games, and believed in Greek gods. Meanwhile, Canadians always spoke the Canadian language, ate Canadian food, played Canadian games, and believed in Canadian gods.

But none of this is true. Canadians don't even speak Canadian—there's no such language. Most Canadians speak English, like people in England, or French, like people in France. Some Canadians speak Inuktitut and Ojibwe, and a few Canadians even speak Greek—because they or their parents came to Canada from Greece. On the other hand, many people in Greece can speak English and French, just like the people in England, France, and Canada.

The situation with gods is as complicated as with languages. Take the Greek gods, for example. Many years ago, there were a lot of Greek gods—you might have heard about some of them, like Zeus, Artemis, and Athena. But today, hardly any Greeks believe in them. Instead, most Greeks believe in Jesus, some believe in Allah, a few believe in Shiva, and many don't believe in any god at all—just like the people in Canada, Nigeria, and India. So it's not true that the world is divided into neat boxes. People in the same country sometimes **speak different languages and believe in different gods**, while people in different countries sometimes speak the same language and believe in the same gods.

The box-people can get quite angry if you tell them this. They say that isn't how things should be. They feel it's a shame that some Greeks eat Italian food, speak the English language, and believe in an Asian god. And they want people to go back in time and behave like "proper" Greeks.

But that's not possible. Because if you go back in time, you realize that all these things keep changing. **None of the countries, languages, or religions of today existed 5,000 years ago.** Back then, there was no Greece, no Canada, no Nigeria, and no India. Nobody spoke English, French, or Greek. And nobody believed in Jesus, Zeus, or Shiva. Sure, there were countries, languages, and religions 5,000 years ago, but they were completely different from the ones we know today. It was only because people moved from place to place and began to think and behave in new ways that eventually our own countries, languages, and religions emerged.

The first Greeks who believed in Jesus, for example, were very different from everyone around them. They believed in a new religion that came from another country and that none of their parents or grandparents had even heard about. For things to change, somebody needs to be the first to accept new stuff—somebody needs to be different.

So if you feel different from the people around you, that's perfectly normal. Most people who lived in your country in ancient times were different from the people living there now. And no matter how hard people try to keep eating the same food, speaking the same language, and believing in the same gods as before, over time all these things change—the gods, the languages, the food, and the people all become different.

But why do things change no matter how hard people try to stay the same? Why do all the people, countries, languages, and religions become different from what they were before? Why did Greeks, for example, stop believing in Zeus and Artemis and begin believing in Jesus? Where do new gods come from and what happens when foreign gods meet?

And even more importantly, what exactly happens when foreign *people* meet? What happens, for example, when you meet someone from a distant country who speaks a foreign language and eats strange food? What happens when you travel across the seas and reach some strange and unfamiliar place? Will you fight or will you get along just fine? How can people who are very different from each other cooperate and even become good friends?

The answer to that question is one of the strangest tales you'll ever hear.

AND it's a true story.

1
DRAGON-PEOPLE, ANT-PEOPLE, AND
WOLF-PEOPLE

CROSSING THE
WATERS OF DEATH

Five thousand years ago, there was no Canada and no Greece, no New York and no New Delhi. But there were already some kingdoms and cities—back then, the biggest city in the world was probably Uruk. Its people spoke the Sumerian language and believed in many gods that are now totally forgotten, like Inanna, An, and Enki.

The Urukians told many interesting stories about their gods and also about their people and their city. **Telling stories was very important because if everyone knew and believed the same stories, it united them and helped them cooperate.** This storytelling makes humans much more powerful than any other animal.

To understand how stories and cooperation make us powerful, you just need to compare us to other animals—to chimpanzees, let's say. Ten chimps can become good friends and help one another find bananas, or hunt a

piglet, or chase away a leopard. But a thousand chimps can't cooperate on anything because they don't know each other well enough. Suppose you cram 1,000 chimps into one place and give them a huge pile of bananas to share. What do you think would happen? Very soon they would be screaming at the top of their voices, running around in a frenzy, or beating each other.

If you could speak chimp language, you might ask one of these chimps: "Why are you fighting? There are enough bananas for everyone."

"Yes," the chimp might reply, "but I've never seen most of these chimps in my life! How can I trust them? Maybe they want to kill me and take all the bananas for themselves."

Humans are different. We discovered long ago how to cooperate in large numbers and how to use stories to build cities and kingdoms. As long as everybody believes in the same story—about the great gods Inanna and Anu, say—even a million humans can cooperate and agree on the rules everybody should follow. For example, people in Uruk told a story about the goddess Inanna making a rule that you shouldn't kill people and shouldn't steal their food. All Urukians believed the story, so they tried to keep these rules, and they could trust other people in Uruk not to kill them or steal their food.

But the most important story that united the Urukians wasn't about the goddess Inanna, or the god An, or any of the other gods. It was about a human hero called Gilgamesh. We know the story of Gilgamesh, because

4

archaeologists who dug in the vicinity of Uruk found ancient tablets from thousands of years ago with Gilgamesh's story written on them.

Once upon a time, said the story, there lived a man called Gilgamesh. He was the bravest man in the world. He became king of Uruk, fought many ogres, and even killed the giant monster Humbaba. One day, Gilgamesh's best friend, Enkidu, died. Gilgamesh sat next to the dead body and watched over it for seven days and nights, until he saw a maggot fall out of his friend's nostril. That little maggot terrified Gilgamesh much more than the monster Humbaba had. Gilgamesh realized that what happened to Enkidu would happen to him too one day. He would be dead, and maggots would eat his body—his strong arms, his brain, and his nose. So what was the point of all his wealth, power, and fame? Why bother pursuing these things when in the end, he would be maggot food? **Gilgamesh decided he must defeat death.**

He left Uruk and traveled from country to country, looking for a way to overcome death. He encountered many dangers, killed many monsters, fought terrible scorpion-people, and finally heard about someone who possibly knew the secret to eternal life. There was a man called Utnapishtim whom Inanna and An and all the other gods loved so much that they gave him the gift of immortality. But Utnapishtim lived beyond a great ocean that nobody could cross because its waters were deadly. **Anyone who touched even one drop from the Waters of Death**

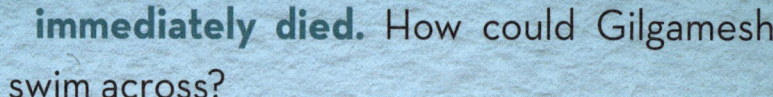

immediately died. How could Gilgamesh swim across?

Luckily, Gilgamesh made a new friend—Urshanabi—who had a boat. Still, even with Urshanabi's boat, how could Gilgamesh row across the Waters of Death without touching the water or being splashed while rowing? Gilgamesh took a shirt and turned it into a sail. He stood inside the boat and used his great body and powerful arms as a mast and yard for the sail. Gilgamesh had just invented the first sail, and he used it to cross the Waters of Death without rowing or touching the water even once.

When Gilgamesh finally met Utnapishtim and asked him for the secret to eternal life, Utnapishtim told him about a miraculous plant that grows at the bottom of a different sea, a sea of life. "If you eat that little plant," said Utnapishtim, "it will make you immortal! But be careful—there's just one such plant in the whole world, and if you lose it, you'll never be able to escape death." Gilgamesh tied heavy stones to his feet and dove to the bottom of the Sea of Life, where he found the plant. He picked it and brought it ashore. But before he ate it, he became distracted for a moment, and a snake stole the plant and swallowed it. The snake shed its skin, became young again, and lived forever after, while Gilgamesh had to return to Uruk empty-handed. Only then did he accept that there was no way to escape death. **No human can**

defeat death. Nobody can stop time. Nobody can prevent change.

Like Gilgamesh, the city of Uruk also eventually died. All its buildings fell apart, and its streets were abandoned. Nobody lives there today except for some spiders, scorpions, and lizards . . . and a few archaeologists digging around in the ruins, hoping to find interesting treasures from ancient times, like the tablets with the text of the Gilgamesh story.

So Uruk no longer exists, but it did leave us some important gifts: not just the story of Gilgamesh but also writing itself. It was in Uruk that people first invented writing. It's thanks to the Urukians that you can now read this book, as well as newspapers, emails, and websites.

BEYOND THE
BORDERS

While Uruk died, other cities and kingdoms were born. Each had its own language, and its own stories about heroes, gods, and the origins of the world. These stories were vital because they helped unite all the people in the kingdom, just as stories about the goddess Inanna and King Gilgamesh helped unite the people of Uruk. But no matter how big a kingdom was, it always had borders, and beyond the borders lived foreigners who believed other stories.

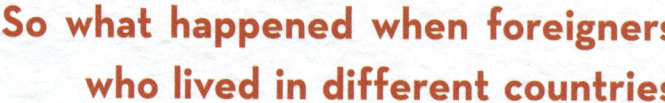

So what happened when foreigners who lived in different countries and believed in different stories met? Did they just fight, or did they find a way to get along? And if they got along, how did they do it?

People are afraid of anything different; they're afraid of foreign people, unknown places, strange foods, and unfamiliar ideas. They might even think, "If we go beyond the borders of our country, some foreigner might kill us." But people are also attracted to faraway places. After all, what you already know can get boring, but the unknown is exciting! So many amazing things could be out there, beyond the horizon. Maybe you'll discover treasures and wonders, taste delicious new foods, and find new friends. Maybe you'll even meet someone who knows the secret to eternal life! That's why, despite our fears, there have always been some people who felt an urge to leave home, cross borders, and travel far.

To understand what happened when people traveled far from home and met foreigners, **let's take a**

journey in our imagination. Imagine a boy called Heraclitus who lived in a city called Ephesus more than 2,200 years ago. He was about to leave his city for the first time and sail with his father across the sea to the distant city of Carthage.

In ancient times, many people went on such journeys, and we know from ancient documents and archaeological discoveries what the cities of Ephesus and Carthage looked like, what kind of ships their people sailed, and what kind of stories their people told. Of course, Heraclitus isn't a real person, and what we're saying about him didn't really happen. Yet the cities of Ephesus and Carthage really existed. Today, they're both heaps of ruins full of spiders, lizards, and archaeologists—just like Uruk. But **2,200 years ago, Carthage was perhaps the biggest city in the whole world**, famous for its market. Merchants from many other cities and countries sailed there to trade, and we know that some merchants made the journey from Ephesus.

Ephesus was also a very important city, famous for its beautiful temple of the goddess Artemis. In those days Ephesus was populated by Greeks who spoke the Greek language. Where would you have to travel to visit the ruins of the beautiful Artemis temple today? To Greece? No, you'd actually need to go to Turkey, because 2,200 years ago there were many Greek cities on what is now the coast of Turkey. Confusing, isn't it? But this is how history works: People, countries, languages, and religions keep changing all the time.

ONE-EYED GIANTS

Imagine that just before leaving Ephesus to sail to Carthage, Heraclitus went to the temple of Artemis to ask the goddess to protect him during his travels. **Artemis was the goddess of nature, wild animals, plants, and children.** People said she could fly through the air, see and hear what was happening hundreds of miles away, and even create animals and plants. They also said she could control terrible diseases, and when she was angry, she was terrifying: She had a magical bow, and if people made her angry, she could shoot them from the sky with arrows of illness. One by one they would fall sick and die. So Heraclitus prayed to Artemis to protect him from diseases, wild animals, storms, and other evils.

The temple of Artemis was the biggest structure Heraclitus had ever seen. In fact, it was the biggest structure almost anyone had ever seen in those days. People came to Ephesus from far and wide just to see the temple of Artemis, and it was considered one of the Seven Wonders of the World. (The other six were other particularly big and beautiful buildings and statues.)

The temple was about 375 feet long, 180 feet wide, and up to 100 feet high—as big as a present-day football field! It was built from shining white marble and had 120 marble columns. Inside, there was a **huge, beautiful statue of the goddess Artemis, covered with gold and silver**. The walls were decorated with many other statues, paintings, and jewels.

After praying to Artemis at the temple, Heraclitus went to say goodbye to his other favorite place in Ephesus—the theater. This was another big building with

lots of marble columns, where actors staged plays about gods and heroes who went on various adventures. Heraclitus loved watching these plays and imagined that one day he too would be a hero and go on an adventure. Maybe someone would even write a play about him!

On his way to the theater, he met a group of his friends. They were looking for him because they wanted to say goodbye. The journey to Carthage and back would take months, and in those days there were no phones or computers, so when someone went on such a journey their friends couldn't talk to them for a long time. **Maybe they would never talk again.**

"Why are you going, Heraclitus?" his friends asked.

"My father's sailing to Carthage today, and he wants me to join him."

"Don't go!" cried one boy. "It's dangerous! Don't you know that the world beyond Ephesus is full of

terrible monsters, like the giant Cyclops? I've heard that Cyclopes are twelve feet tall, they have just one eye in the middle of the head, and they eat people!"

"I've heard that too!" shouted a red-haired girl. "And I've also heard that there are witches who lure you to their home and let you eat the most delicious food, but they put a magic potion in the food, and when you eat it, you become a pig!"

"That's right!" the first boy agreed, getting so excited his nose began running a little. "And there are Sirens! They're seabirds with human heads who live on sharp rocks that lurk just beneath the waves. When they see a passing ship, they raise their human heads and start to sing the most bewitching songs. Nobody who hears their song can resist it. You sail nearer and nearer to listen . . . and *wham!* You hit the sharp rocks, your ship breaks up, and then the Sirens attack and rip you to pieces!"

"I'm not afraid of all that!" replied Heraclitus, even though he was starting to feel a little uneasy. "If the Cyclopes or Sirens come to eat me, I'll take my sword and stick it in their belly!"

"Don't be silly," said another girl. "There are no Cyclopes or Sirens. **Those are just fairy tales** people tell about places they never visited. I guess people in other countries tell scary fairy tales about us too, saying Ephesus is full of giants and witches who eat humans. But actually, wherever you go in the world, you find humans just like us."

The girl was right, of course. Cyclopes, Sirens, and other monsters existed only in the stories ancient people invented and told one another. One particularly good storyteller from those days was called Homer, and he composed two very famous stories: the *Iliad* and the *Odyssey*. In the *Iliad*, he told the story of an army of Greek warriors, led by the heroes Agamemnon, Menelaus, Achilles, and Odysseus, who conquered the city of Troy. In the *Odyssey*, he described how Odysseus later traveled around the world and met Cyclopes, Sirens, sorcerers, and witches. **You've probably heard at least some of**

these tales, and if you want, you can still read the *Iliad* and the *Odyssey* in their entirety today.

"Maybe," agreed the boy with the runny nose, "Cyclopes and Sirens are just imaginary stories people invented. But it's still dangerous to go to foreign places. Foreigners might be human, but they're as dangerous as Cyclopes!"

"Right!" added the red-haired girl. "I've heard the world is full of enemies and pirates and—worst of all—Romans! They'll rob you and kill you, Heraclitus."

"But I'm going to Carthage," protested Heraclitus. "There are no Romans in Carthage. Just Carthaginians."

"Still," said Runny-Nose, "it'll be dangerous for you in Carthage! They have very strange rules there, and because you don't know their rules, you could break one and they'll punish you. Maybe they have a rule that you're not allowed to sneeze in the street, so you just do a harmless little sneeze, and they put you in jail or kill you. And you couldn't even ask them about their strange rules because you don't speak their language. Here in Ephesus everyone speaks Greek, but in Carthage nobody knows Greek. They speak a language called Phoenician. You don't know a single word of Phoenician! How will you cope, Heraclitus?"

"And what will you eat there?" added Red-Hair. "**They probably have strange and disgusting food.** I've heard they eat rotten fish!"

"And they don't believe in the goddess Artemis!" exclaimed Runny-Nose. "We built Artemis the most

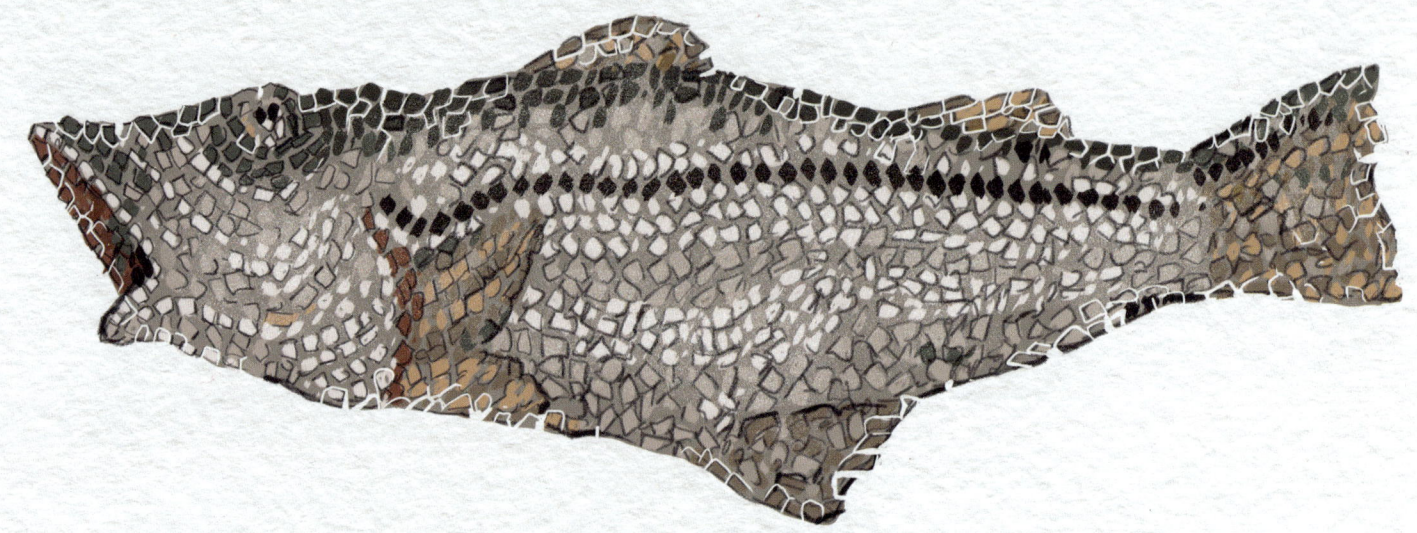

magnificent temple in the world, with marble pillars and gold statues, so she protects us. But in Carthage they don't have any temples for Artemis. When you are in Carthage, how will you pray to Artemis to protect you?"

"And they don't have a theater there!" shouted Red-Hair. "You know how much you like the theater, Heraclitus, and all the latest plays. But apparently there are no theaters at all in Carthage. They don't even know what theater is. If they don't kill you for sneezing in the street, and if you don't die from eating rotten fish, you'll probably be bored to death!"

"I am not scared of all that," said Heraclitus. "You're just finding excuses for me not to go. First you said the world is full of one-eyed giants; now you're saying they're just humans who eat rotten fish and have no theater. I guess you have no idea what you're talking about. I want to see Carthage with my own eyes. I've heard it's the biggest city in the world. If they don't believe in Artemis, I want to know what gods they do believe in. And if they don't have theater, maybe I can teach them about it."

STORIES OF
ORIGIN

We know that, despite fears like those of Heraclitus's friends, lots of people made long sea voyages in those days, and not just from Ephesus to Carthage—they traveled between numerous destinations. We know this because **we've found stories and poems that ancient people wrote about these journeys**, and we've even found the wrecks of some of their ships.

In 1982, one such ship was found off the coast of Turkey, near a place called Uluburun, not far from Ephesus. The ship's wreckage was first spotted by a young fisherman called Mehmet Çakir, who was diving in the sea to look for sponges. He noticed some strange objects on the seabed and told the director of a local archaeology museum. A team of professional underwater archaeologists was sent to search the place. Almost 165 feet underwater, they found the ancient ship . . . and all kinds of fantastic treasure.

When it sank, the Uluburun ship was laden with ten tons of copper, mostly from the nearby island of Cyprus, and one ton of tin, some of which came from Uzbekistan, thousands of miles away. It also carried tools and weapons: sickles, chisels, a saw, a plowshare, arrowheads, spearheads, maces, daggers, four swords, and two axes. There was blackwood from Africa on board, part of an

elephant tusk, several ostrich eggshells, and more than a dozen hippopotamus teeth. The archaeologists identified food remnants as well: olives, figs, almonds, nuts, grapes, pomegranates, and spices like coriander seed, cumin, and sumac. Finally, the ship carried lots of jewelry too. There were gold pendants, silver bracelets, shell rings, amber and glass beads, two cosmetic boxes made of ivory, a tortoise shell that once served as the sound box of a lute, and **a trumpet carved from a hippopotamus tooth**.

The archaeologists found so many interesting things in the wrecked ship, they had to make more than 22,000 dives to bring them all to the surface! It sounds like a perfect job—scuba diving in the sea to look for ancient treasure.

Why did the Uluburun ship sink? It wasn't because of singing Sirens or one-eyed giants, but probably because of a storm. Even though monsters didn't exist, the world was still a dangerous place. Runny-Nose and Red-Hair did

have some good reasons to be afraid of traveling. So, when Heraclitus boarded his father's ship, the *Theseus*, he looked a bit worried.

"What's the matter, Heraclitus?" asked a sailor called Jason, who was just a little older than Heraclitus and was dressed in a yellow sheep-fleece coat. "You look a bit scared."

"I'm not scared!" said Heraclitus, putting on a brave face.

"But it's normal to be scared," said Jason. "I was *terrified* on my first big voyage!"

"You were?" asked Heraclitus, surprised. He always thought sailors weren't afraid of anything.

"Sure I was," Jason replied. **"People told me the world's full of dragons, witches, and pirates, and that if the Cyclopes didn't eat me, the foreigners sure would!"**

"And was any of it true?" asked Heraclitus.

"Some of it. There are no Cyclopes or witches, but I did meet some dangerous foreigners who tried to rob me and kill me. On the other hand, I also met really nice foreigners who became my best friends. And some of them are right here on the *Theseus*!"

"What?!" cried Heraclitus, looking around suspiciously. "You mean the other sailors?"

"Yes. Not all of them are from Ephesus, you know. Here, come meet my mate Oedipus. He's from Thebes."

"What kind of a name is Oedipus?" Heraclitus muttered.

"Don't ask . . ." replied Oedipus. "My mother named me after some old king in a play she liked."

"Really?" asked Heraclitus. "I once saw a play about Thebes—there was a dragon in it!"

"That's right!" said Oedipus. "There used to be a dragon in Thebes, but that was a long time ago. When the dragon lived there, no human dared approach the place. One day a prince named Cadmus came to the area from the land of Phoenicia. The dragon killed Cadmus's friends, but Cadmus fought and killed it. Then the goddess Athena appeared and told Cadmus to take the dragon's teeth and sow them in the ground. Out of the teeth sprouted fully armed warriors who attacked Cadmus with their swords. Cadmus tossed a stone among them, and they immediately left him alone and began fighting among themselves. Almost all of them were killed, but Cadmus convinced the last five to stop fighting and help him build a new city. That's how Thebes was founded. We Thebans are descended from the dragon. We're dragon-men!"

"Interesting story," another sailor called Achilles jumped in. "But tell me, if **Thebes was founded by Cadmus and his five dragon-men**, how exactly did they have any kids? You didn't say anything about dragon-women."

"Give me a break, Achilles," said Oedipus. "At least I'm not named after a guy who couldn't even handle a scratch on his heel. You're just jealous that you're not a dragon-man!"

"Ha, why would I be jealous?" laughed Achilles, puffing up his chest. "I'm named after the greatest hero who

ever lived, and I was born on the most wonderful island in the world—Aegina! And do you know where we Aeginians came from?"

"No," said Heraclitus, shaking his head.

"Well, one day the goddess Hera was angry with the people of Aegina, so she sent a plague and killed every last human on the island."

"But how does that explain where you Aeginians came from?" asked Heraclitus.

"I haven't finished," Achilles said irritably. "It isn't polite to interrupt someone in the middle of a story. Where was I? Yes, the island was empty. So the god **Zeus performed a miracle** and transformed the ants of Aegina into humans! That's why they call us Myrmidons—it means 'ant-people'—and why we're as fierce as ants and as loyal to our king as ants are to their ant king."

"Ants don't have a king!" laughed a third sailor who had a long beard. "They have a queen. And I never heard anybody but you say ants are fierce. Why, you can just step on them. And are you sure someone can turn ants into humans? That would be difficult, even for a god."

"Don't you dare step on an ant, Jonah!" Achilles warned the bearded sailor. "Or I'll show you how fierce we ant-people are!"

"Cool it," said Jonah. "I'm not afraid of you, Achilles. I'm protected by the greatest god in the world—the god of my people, our big father who lives up in the sky. I think of him as my Sky Father. At first, my people were slaves in the land of Egypt, but then the Sky Father rescued us. He rained frogs on the Egyptians and made the sun disappear, and we escaped. The Egyptians came after us with lots of soldiers and horses, but the Sky Father made a miracle and parted the sea, and we crossed the sea to a wonderful land called Canaan. When the Egyptians tried to follow us, the Sky Father closed the sea on them, and they all drowned! And that's where we Jews came from!"

"I was in Egypt three times," interrupted a sailor called Gaius, "and nobody there had ever heard this story. Don't you think the Egyptians would remember something like frogs raining from the sky or the sea parting?"

"Maybe they forgot," said Jonah. "It was a very long time ago."

"Well," boasted Gaius, "nobody ever forgets a visit by my people, and everyone knows where we came from. Long ago in a city called Alba Longa, **a princess gave birth to twin brothers, Romulus and Remus**. Their father was Mars, the god of war. The king of Alba noticed that there was something different and magical about these twins, and he was afraid they would take over his kingdom one

day. So he ordered his soldiers to take the twins and throw them into the River Tiber. But the babies washed ashore, and a she-wolf found them. She took them to her den, and instead of eating them . . . she fed them with her own milk! When Romulus and Remus grew up, they killed the evil king, and then founded a new city—Rome!"

"You're Roman!" cried Heraclitus in alarm.

"Yes, I am," said Gaius, and he snarled like a wolf.

All the sailors laughed and told Heraclitus not to take Gaius seriously. "He's just trying to scare you. Gaius is Roman, but he's the nicest person you'll ever meet. He wouldn't even step on an ant."

"That's right," said Gaius, looking more serious now. "I like ants, like my buddy Achilles here. **People don't care about them, but if you look carefully, you'll see that they really suffer if someone steps on them.**"

"So how come you ended up on this ship?" asked Heraclitus. "And you can speak Greek? I thought Romans spoke Latin."

"Well," said Gaius, "I was a Roman soldier, what they call a legionnaire, and I saw a lot of violence during my time in the army. I just couldn't stand it any longer. Somebody told me about a faraway country called India where some people are so opposed to violence, they don't even step on ants. So I decided to travel to India and meet these people. But pirates attacked my ship and killed everyone except me. I jumped overboard and clung to a piece of wood for three days, convinced I was going to die. The gods were probably punishing me for all the bad things I did in the army. Then your father passed by on the *Theseus*, and he rescued me. He and the other sailors were so nice that I decided to stay on the *Theseus*. That was ten years ago, so I've had plenty of time to pick up some Greek. But I still want to continue my travels and reach India someday."

"And you, Jonah, how come you speak Greek?" asked Heraclitus. "I thought Jews spoke Hebrew."

"Same story, basically. I was traveling from the port of Jaffa to Iberia, when my ship sank in a storm. But a big fish saved my life."

"A fish!" cried Heraclitus. "Is that a true story?"

"Yes, it is. You see, I managed to swim to a desert island, but there was nothing to eat there, so I almost starved to death. Then I caught this big fish and ate it. So you see, that fish saved my life. Without it, I would have died. I'm pretty sure it was the Sky Father who sent me that fish. A week later the *Theseus* passed by and picked me up. Like Gaius, I stuck around and learned Greek."

"And you two." Heraclitus turned to Oedipus and Achilles. "How come you know Greek so well?"

"What a question!" cried the Theban and the Aeginian together. "People speak Greek in Thebes and Aegina too! Even better than in Ephesus!"

THE SHIP AND **THE MARKET**

Just like the sailors aboard the *Theseus*, humans can learn to speak many languages. You probably learn a second language in school, or maybe your family speaks a different language at home. But just speaking the same language doesn't make people the same, and it doesn't mean they must belong to the same country. Today, people in Mexico, Argentina, and Cuba all speak Spanish, but these are still three different countries. Similarly, ancient people in Ephesus, Thebes, and Aegina all spoke Greek, but there

wasn't a single big Greek country to which they all belonged. **Back then the Greeks were divided into hundreds of independent tribes, cities, islands, and kingdoms.** Each believed in different stories and obeyed different leaders. Sometimes they even fought each other.

For example, you might have heard of the big war that the Greek city of Athens fought against the Greek city of Sparta. It was called the Peloponnesian War, and gradually almost all the other Greeks—in Thebes, Aegina, and elsewhere—joined one of the two sides. The fact that both Athenians and Spartans spoke Greek didn't prevent this terrible war. Other people, like Jews and Romans, could also learn Greek, but this was no guarantee that Jews, Romans, and Greeks would always live in peace.

If language wasn't enough to unite people, what could help the dragon-people from Thebes and the ant-people from Aegina get along with the people of Ephesus? And how could they also trust the wolf-people from Rome and the Jews and the Carthaginians?

These questions might have bothered Heraclitus as he sailed toward Carthage.

"Maybe on a small ship like the *Theseus*," thought Heraclitus, "different people could get along because there's just a handful of them, and they have time to get to know one another personally. My father chose to have only very nice sailors like Gaius on the *Theseus*, and having been together for several years,

they all became friends. But what will happen when we get to Carthage? I've heard that **more foreigners come to the market in Carthage than anywhere else in the world**, and most of them visit for only a few days. Surely, they don't have time to learn each other's languages, hear each other's stories, and become friends. So how can they get along? Will all these foreigners attack and rob me, or do the Carthaginians have some secret that helps thousands of foreigners to trust each other?"

Let's leave Heraclitus and his questions for a while—we'll hear the end of his story later. Instead, let's come ashore in Carthage to explore its secret.

2
THE SECRET OF
THE MARKET

THE LOST
CITY

Do you ever fantasize that one day you'll travel to a distant jungle or desert and find a lost city full of long-forgotten temples and hidden treasures? This fantasy can actually come true because **there really are lost cities in different parts of the world**. Carthage is one of them.

Carthage was built in North Africa, on the coast of the Mediterranean Sea. Today the country around it is called Tunisia. If you travel to Tunisia and visit Carthage, you won't see much, just some ruins, broken marble columns, scattered stone blocks, and lots of pottery shards, along with some spiders, scorpions, and lizards. But if you were allowed to dig up the ground, you might discover temples and palaces, beautiful statues, ancient jewels and swords, golden crowns, and silver bracelets. For in its glory days, **Carthage was perhaps the biggest and richest city in the world**.

Carthage was founded about 2,800 years ago by Phoenician people who sailed from Phoenicia to North Africa. By the time Heraclitus was traveling there, half a million Carthaginians lived in the city of Carthage itself, and thousands more lived in the surrounding small towns and villages.

Let's join two imaginary Carthaginian kids from one of the small villages—Hanniba'al and his sister Saponiba'al—who came to the city for the first time to see their older sister who lived there. They also decided to visit the famous temples of the great god Ba'al and the mother goddess Tanit, the chief gods of Carthage. Since they'd never been to Carthage before and it was a very big city, Hanniba'al and Saponiba'al quickly got lost in the maze of streets. Luckily for them, they met a local girl called Batba'al and asked her for help.

"Excuse me," said Hanniba'al in the nicest voice he could muster, "could you please show us the way to the temples of Ba'al and Tanit? I think we're just a little bit lost."

"I'm happy to help!" replied Batba'al. "And don't feel bad about getting lost. I see strangers losing their way here almost every day. I'm Batba'al, by the way, but you can call me Bati."

"Nice to meet you, Bati," said Saponiba'al. "I'm Saponiba'al, but you can call me Sapo. And this is my brother Hanniba'al . . . erm, you can call him Hanniba'al. He doesn't like it when people shorten his name."

"That's right!" said Hanniba'al. "I like my name just as it is because I'm named after the famous general Hanniba'al!"

"Oh, I've heard of him." Batba'al nodded.

"Everybody's heard of him!" cried Hanniba'al. "**He crossed the snowy Alp mountains with the whole Carthaginian army and his war elephants**—something nobody dared do before him! And he won a great victory at the battle of Cannae, defeating sixteen Roman legions all at once!"

Saponiba'al rolled her eyes. "Yes, brother, you keep telling that story, but you always forget to mention that in the end he lost the war. . . ."

As they walked through the crowded streets, Saponiba'al and Hanniba'al were amazed by what they saw. In their village, everyone lived in small houses or huts and had to walk to the village well to get water. In Carthage many people lived in high apartment blocks, and there were even pipes that brought water to the upper floors! The children were even more astonished by the sheer number of people.

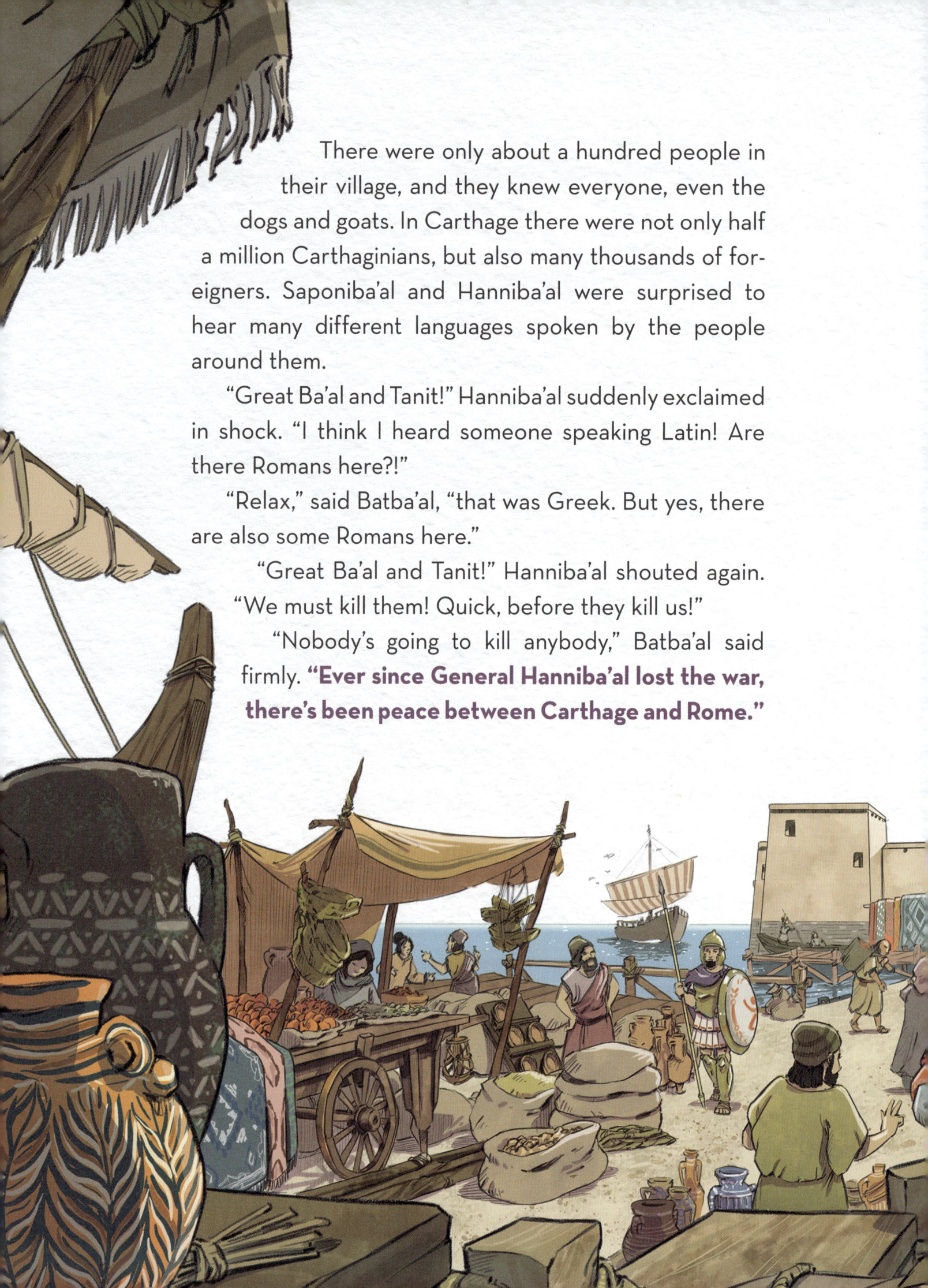

There were only about a hundred people in their village, and they knew everyone, even the dogs and goats. In Carthage there were not only half a million Carthaginians, but also many thousands of foreigners. Saponiba'al and Hanniba'al were surprised to hear many different languages spoken by the people around them.

"Great Ba'al and Tanit!" Hanniba'al suddenly exclaimed in shock. "I think I heard someone speaking Latin! Are there Romans here?!"

"Relax," said Batba'al, "that was Greek. But yes, there are also some Romans here."

"Great Ba'al and Tanit!" Hanniba'al shouted again. "We must kill them! Quick, before they kill us!"

"Nobody's going to kill anybody," Batba'al said firmly. **"Ever since General Hanniba'al lost the war, there's been peace between Carthage and Rome."**

"Tell me, Bati," Saponiba'al asked quickly, before Hanniba'al could complain more about the Romans, "why are all these foreigners here? Do they come to visit the temples of Ba'al and Tanit?"

"A few do," replied Batba'al. "But most come for the market. You can buy anything in the Carthage market. Even an elephant."

Batba'al was right. The Carthage market was the biggest in the world, and it attracted foreigners from hundreds and even thousands of miles away. Arab and Jewish merchants came to Carthage, bringing spices like pepper and cinnamon. Greek merchants brought the best wine from Greece, as well as perfume, pots, and plates. Merchants from Egypt, Persia, and India arrived with gold and silver jewels, fine

textiles, glass, and papyrus. **And yes, you could even buy elephants, which were brought to Carthage from the African savannah.**

"Elephants!" cried Hanniba'al. "I love elephants! General Hanniba'al rode an elephant almost to the gates of Rome!"

"What's that strange smell?" Saponiba'al asked, hoping to change the subject.

"That's garum," replied Batba'al. "Rotten fish sauce."

"Rotten fish sauce? People eat that?!" exclaimed Saponiba'al and Hanniba'al simultaneously.

"It's the most delicious thing in the world!" explained Batba'al. "The best garum comes from Spain. They take the intestines from little fish, mix them with salt, and leave them in the sun for a couple of months. Merchants from Carthage go to Spain, bring entire jars full of garum back here, and then other merchants come to Carthage from other lands to buy this garum. Do you want to try some?"

"No thanks," they both said. "We think we'll skip the rotten fish. We prefer olive oil."

"In that case, you're in the right place!" Batba'al smiled. "You must visit the olive oil

shop on the next street. They get their oil from a Greek merchant who knows where to find the best olive oil in the world! I'm telling you—you can get anything in the Carthage market. **That's why people come here from all over the world**, and that's why Carthage is the richest city in the world."

"So they come here to sell their olive oil and cinnamon and elephants," said Hanniba'al. "They buy rotten fish sauce and textiles, and then they go home to Greece or Arabia or wherever?"

"Most of the time," Batba'al confirmed. "But sometimes they stay longer, maybe even their whole life. That's what my grandfather did."

"Your grandfather?!" asked Hanniba'al, his eyes opening wide in surprise.

"Yes. His name's Heraclitus. When he was a kid about our age, he came to the Carthage market with his father from the Greek city of Ephesus. But he fell in love with a Carthaginian girl he met at the market—my grandmother—and stayed."

"Great Ba'al and Tanit!" cried Hanniba'al—he did that a lot. "You tricked us. You're Greek! Why do you have a Carthaginian name, then?"

"I'm not Greek," insisted Batba'al. "I'm Carthaginian just like

37

you. I believe in Ba'al and Tanit, just like you. I don't even speak any Greek, except for a few curse words I learned from my grandfather. He usually speaks Phoenician, but when he gets really upset, he still curses in Greek."

Hanniba'al calmed down a little and said, "Well, at least you're Greek and not Roman. The Greeks are our friends. They also hate the Romans."

"Great Ba'al and Tanit!" cried Batba'al. "I'm not Greek! Just because my grandfather came from across the sea doesn't mean I am a foreigner."

"You know," said Saponiba'al, looking Hanniba'al right in the eye, "our grandma once told me that actually all Carthaginians originally came from across the sea. She said this country once belonged to a local Numidian tribe, but then a queen called Elissa led an expedition here from the land of Phoenicia. When Elissa and her Phoenician people arrived, the king of the local tribe, Iarbas, wouldn't let them stay. He told them they could have only as much land as the skin of the single ox can cover. So you know what Queen Elissa did?"

"What?" asked Hanniba'al.

"Elissa killed an ox, skinned it, cut the hide into tiny strips, and surrounded a huge territory with these strips. That's how we got this land and built Carthage on it."

"Now that you mention it," said Hanniba'al, "I remember Grandma telling me that story. So does that mean we're all foreigners who once came from another country?"

ON TREES AND HUMANS

It isn't always easy to know who's a foreigner and who's a local. **People sometimes move from country to country.** Foreigners might settle down, and they might marry locals. And while no miracle can turn dragon's teeth into warriors or ants into humans, time can gradually turn foreigners into locals.

Saponiba'al and Hanniba'al were silent as they thought about Queen Elissa and her story. Did it mean they were all foreigners? Finally, Batba'al interrupted their thoughts: "My grandfather Heraclitus likes to say that we humans aren't trees—we don't have deep roots that hold us in one place all our lives. Humans have legs, so we move around. And we invented carts and boats and ships that allow us to move around even more. And whenever we move, we become a little different."

"What do you mean by 'different'?" asked Hanniba'al.

"Well, it's like what happened to my grandfather's ship, the *Theseus*. It once belonged to *his* father, who built it in Ephesus, but my grandfather got it as a wedding present when he married my grandmother and settled in Carthage. A year after the wedding, one of the oars on the *Theseus* broke, and my grandfather replaced it with a new one from the Carthage market. **Would you say his ship was still the *Theseus*, or did it become a different ship?**"

"It was obviously still the *Theseus*," replied Hanniba'al confidently. "Replacing just one oar doesn't change the ship."

"Then the following year, another oar broke and he replaced that one too. Was it still the *Theseus*?" asked Batba'al.

"Obviously."

"The third year the sail got torn in a storm, and my grandfather bought a new sail in the market. What do you think now?"

"Still the *Theseus*," said Hanniba'al, with a little less confidence.

"The following year my grandfather noticed that one plank in the ship's hull had started to rot, so he changed that plank. Still the same ship?"

"Eh, I think so, yes. It's just one plank."

"The next year he replaced a second plank."

"Still the *Theseus*," said Hanniba'al, beginning to think that Batba'al was the smartest girl he ever met.

"Every year he replaced another plank, until only one plank from the original ship remained. Finally, even that plank broke, and my grandfather put a new one in its place. Is it still the *Theseus* now?"

"I don't think so," Hanniba'al said hesitatingly. "There's nothing left of the original ship from Ephesus, right? Not the oars, not the sail, not even any of the planks. How can it be the same ship?"

"Then tell me, Hanniba'al," asked Batba'al, "when exactly did it stop being the *Theseus* and become a different ship? When the first oar was changed? When the first plank was changed? When the last plank was changed?"

"That's a good question, Bati. I don't know where to draw the line."

"Well, it's like that with people. **It's not easy to draw the lines between different groups of people**, and people often move across these lines. Even a foreigner from a distant land can become family. When my grandfather came from Ephesus on the *Theseus*, he was Greek. I, his granddaughter, am Carthaginian. Just as it isn't easy to say when exactly the *Theseus* changed into a new ship, it isn't easy to say when exactly a Greek turns into a Carthaginian!"

"I hear what you're saying, Bati," said Hanniba'al, and he smiled. "Once people from different lands start mixing in

the market, it's no longer easy to be sure who's a foreigner and who's a local. But there's one thing I don't understand. How do foreigners mix in the market in the first place? How do they supply one another with oars, sails, robes, olive oil, rotten fish sauce, and even elephants? They come from different countries, speak different languages, worship different gods, and believe different stories. So **how can they agree on anything or trust one another?**"

"Good question," said Batba'al. She thought a little before going on. "I think it's because, even though they don't have the same language or gods, there's still one thing they all trust and they all agree upon. It's one of the strangest and most important things in the world."

"What is it?" Hanniba'al asked.

"Let's go into a shop and I'll show you. Say, is there anything one of you needs now that you're at the market?"

"Yes!" Saponiba'al piped up. "My shoes are torn. My uncle made them for me last year, and to be honest, he isn't the best shoemaker. Do you think someone in the market would agree to make me a new pair?"

"Of course! There are lots of shoemakers in the market. Let's go to my favorite one, Wen-Amun. He's from Egypt, and he's a shoe genius! But I should warn you, he isn't a very nice person."

"Are you sure he'll agree to make me a pair of shoes?"

"I think we can persuade him," replied Batba'al with a wink.

THE CLEVEREST
INVENTION EVER

When they entered Wen-Amun the shoemaker's shop, Saponiba'al and Hanniba'al were amazed by all the pretty shoes there. One pair in particular caught Saponiba'al's eye. She pointed at them and asked the shoemaker in her friendliest voice, "Please, sir, could you make me a pair of shoes just like those?"

"Mmm . . ." said Wen-Amun, "you have expensive taste, young lady. Those shoes are made from Egyptian leather that I bring all the way from Crocodile City in the Nile Valley. And the buckle is pure Cypriot copper! They're the best of the best!"

"Great! When my uncle made my last pair, he said I deserve only the best."

"And how much did your uncle charge you for them?" asked Wen-Amun.

"What do you mean, 'charge'? In our village, people give each other what they need without asking for anything in return."

"But this is not your village, and I'm not your uncle. I'm also not sure you can afford the shoes."

"Oh, I get it. You want me to give you something in return for the shoes?"

"Yes, that's how it works in the market."

"Let's see," said Saponiba'al, and she began rummaging through her bag.

"That's a nice bag you have there," said Wen-Amun. "I'll trade you the shoes for the bag."

"What?!" cried Saponiba'al in alarm. "My grandmother made this bag for me just before she died. She even knitted flowers and birds on it. No, I won't give this bag away for anything. But look, I've got some nice seashells we collected this morning on the beach. I'll gladly give you those."

The shoemaker frowned.

"I also have a half-eaten loaf of bread."

The shoemaker frowned even more.

"I've got five figs. They're from our orchard in the village. They're very sweet and juicy!"

"You really think a pair of leather shoes is worth just five figs?"

"If you want, I can bring you more figs. No problem. We have a whole orchard of them."

"And **how am I supposed to know how many figs a pair of shoes is worth?** A hundred? Two hundred? A

thousand? Besides, I don't even like figs. If I eat too many, I get a stomachache."

"So don't eat them all yourself. You can give some to other people. Like, if you need a haircut, you can give some figs to the barber."

"And how many figs does a haircut cost these days? And what if the barber doesn't like figs either?"

"Maybe you can keep the figs until you find a barber who likes them."

"Are you trying to fool me?" the shoemaker snapped angrily. "My shoes will last years, but your figs will probably rot in a few days. Forget it. I'm not selling you shoes for figs. Get out of my shop; you're wasting my time!"

"Wait," said Batba'al, and she drew a shiny gold coin from her pocket. "Would you sell us the shoes for this?"

"Now you're talking!" The shoemaker beamed, and he gladly took the coin from Batba'al's hand. "The shoes are yours!"

He carefully measured Saponiba'al's feet, made some marks on a brand-new sheet of leather, and told her to come back the next day to pick up the new shoes.

Saponiba'al was overjoyed but also a bit confused.

"What was that shiny thing you gave the shoemaker?" she asked. "And why was he so quick to sell us the shoes? He made such a big fuss about my figs but didn't ask any questions about your ... your ... What was that thing, anyway?"

"That thing is called money. Here, I have another one for you," said Batba'al, handing Saponiba'al a gold coin.

"What you now have in your hand is **maybe the cleverest thing anyone ever invented**!"

"Oh, I heard about this money thing before," said Saponiba'al, turning the coin this way and that. "My parents talked about it the other day. But I never actually saw one. We don't use it in our village. Look, Hanniba'al! It has the image of the goddess Tanit on it! And a horse on the other side!"

"Amazing!" exclaimed Hanniba'al. "Say, Bati, how does this money work? It's very pretty, for sure. But why was that grumpy Egyptian shoemaker so eager to have it? I mean, what's it good for?"

THE STORY OF MONEY

Hanniba'al's last question was a very important one. It's a question many people still ask today. It's not easy to understand how money works, but almost everything that happens in the world is somehow connected to money. Perhaps your parents work very hard for many hours each day to get money—it's what most grown-ups do for most of their lives. And when you ask them for anything like new shoes or a trip to an amusement park, they might say, "Sorry, but we don't have enough money."

You probably use money almost every day too. You use it to buy snacks, perhaps you get it as a present for your birthday, and you could be saving it up to buy something special like a skateboard.

Money was the secret to the Carthage market, and of many other big markets in history. **Money is what made it possible for large numbers of foreigners who'd never met before to get along**, cooperate with one another, and agree on how much things cost. But what exactly is money?

In different times and places, people invented many different kinds of money. But they have all been based on

the same principle: creating something that people always want so everybody would always agree to sell shoes, figs, or skateboards for it. When the Carthage market was first established, people used lumps of precious metals like gold and silver as money. A few centuries later, people in Ephesus and several nearby cities were the first to think of minting beautiful coins out of these metal lumps. Then Greek merchants like Heraclitus and his father brought this idea to Carthage, and the Carthaginians began minting their own coins.

People in other countries had other kinds of money. In many parts of East Africa and South Asia, for example, people used cowrie shells as money. Cowrie shells are a particularly pretty kind of seashell found on certain islands and coasts in Africa and Asia. In these lands people could sell rice, soya beans, or pigs for cowrie shells. They could go to the market with a bag full of cowrie shells and use them to buy shoes, pots, haircuts, or anything else they needed.

In modern times, most countries began using colorful paper banknotes as money. You probably use banknotes

too. But nowadays **most money in the world isn't metal coins or paper banknotes**, and it certainly isn't seashells. Do you know what most money is made of today?

It's made of electronic information in computers. If someone has a million dollars, they usually don't hoard a million one-dollar bills in their house, or 100,000 ten-dollar bills. Instead, there's a file on a big computer in some bank that says they own a million dollars. And if you want to buy shoes for $100, you just transfer some of those electronic dollars to the shop's account. You can do it with a credit card or with a few clicks on your computer or your smartphone, and even if the shop is in a distant foreign country, it will get your money within seconds. After you transfer the money to the shop, your file in the bank's computer says you have $100 less, while the shop's computer file gets $100 more. People now buy shoes, bicycles, houses, and even spaceships from all over the world just by moving electronic money between computers.

All these forms of money have been very useful because they make it easier to buy and sell things, from shoes to spaceships. Instead of going to the market with a cart full of figs, you can take just a little purse full of coins and banknotes or a smartphone full of electronic money. And you don't have to worry about your money rotting. Figs rot easily, but it's much harder for coins, banknotes, credit cards, and electronic money to rot.

Perhaps most importantly, money makes it easy to trade because everyone always wants money. Saponiba'al had difficulty buying shoes with figs because Wen-Amun the shoemaker didn't like figs. But if you walk into a shop with money, you can be sure that even the grumpiest shoemaker will want it.

We're so used to money, it seems obvious that everybody wants it. But this is actually very strange. **No other animal would ever be interested in money!** If you let an elephant choose between a single fig, a suitcase filled with a million one-dollar bills, and a chest full of glittering gold coins, the elephant would obviously go for the

fig. So why do humans value paper banknotes and gold coins?

It's because of the stories we hear about them. People tell us that money has a certain value . . . and we believe it. Money isn't the gold or banknotes or seashells it's made of. Money is a story. When you come across money for the first time in life, someone shows you a coin or a banknote and tells you a story about it. "You see this thing?" they say. "It's very valuable! It is worth 1,000 figs! If you want one of these coins or banknotes, you'll have to work long and hard to get it." And if you believe the story—and everybody around you believes the story—then that coin or banknote really becomes valuable.

Money is actually the most successful story ever told because it's the only story almost all people in the world believe. Not everyone believes that dragon's teeth can become warriors or that the god Zeus can turn ants into humans. But everyone believes in money, and everyone believes that money can turn figs into elephants: If you have enough figs, you can sell them for money, and then use the money to buy an elephant.

It's the story *about* the gold coins—rather than the coins themselves—that allowed thousands of foreigners to get along well in the Carthage market. Thanks to the story about money, even people who didn't agree on any other story could agree on how much a pair of shoes or an elephant cost. As long as different people all used the

same money, they could cooperate, selling each other figs, shoes, and elephants.

CONNECTING **FOREIGNERS**

But what made the story of money so convincing? You might think people started believing it because the first money was very beautiful. Ancient coins, for example, were made of shiny gold and silver and were covered in handsome images of gods and temples. Modern banknotes are also decorated with colorful images of gods and temples or of important people and famous buildings. There are also short texts written on coins and banknotes, perhaps a little poem or a legend about kings and gods. Modern American dollars, for example, have text in English saying "In God We Trust" and text in Latin saying "E pluribus unum," which means "Out of many, one." What do you think this means? It implies that the story about the American god and the American dollar unites many people into one country: the United States.

In addition to all these images, poems, and texts, it's common to cover money with long, complicated numbers that look very impressive. The electronic money many people use today doesn't have any pictures of gods on it,

but it has a lot of very complicated numbers to help people trust it.

Do you have any coins or banknotes at home? Have a really good look at one. You'll be amazed how many images, words, and numbers people manage to squeeze onto such a small space.

But that doesn't explain why even complete foreigners who couldn't agree on anything else managed to agree on the story of money. After all, not everyone in the Carthage market could read the text on the coins: They were written in Phoenician, and not everyone understood Phoenician. Similarly, not everyone believed in the goddess Tanit, who was often depicted on Carthaginian coins. Actually, in the Carthage market you could use a lot of coins that weren't Carthaginian. You could use coins from Athens, which showed the goddess Athena rather than Tanit. You could use coins from Rome, which showed the goddess Venus. So, clearly, it wasn't a story about a

particular goddess that made people believe in money. What was it, then?

To answer this question, let's go back to Saponiba'al and Wen-Amun. When Saponiba'al went back to the market to pick up her beautiful new shoes, she asked Wen-Amun, "Why do you want these gold coins so much that you're willing to work a whole day just to get a single one? My brother and I think this is very strange! We've thought about it since yesterday, but we can't figure it out."

"When I first came to the market," Wen-Amun replied, "I was just like you. I thought it was very strange that people wanted these coins so much. I didn't understand it at all. **The coins are pretty, but you can't eat them or drink them, right?**"

"Exactly!"

"They have images of great gods on them," continued Wen-Amun, "but I don't believe in these gods. I believe in the Egyptian gods Amun, Osiris, and Isis, while most coins here have images of the Carthaginian goddess Tanit or the Athenian goddess Athena. The people in the market told me all kinds of wonderful stories about these coins, but I hardly understood what they were saying, because I didn't speak Phoenician well."

"So why did you start liking the coins?" Saponiba'al persisted.

"Well, even though I didn't understand what people were saying, I could see with my own eyes what they were doing. I noticed that almost everybody else in the market

really wanted these coins. I saw people selling figs for coins. Then I saw people selling huge watermelons for coins. I saw barbers giving haircuts for coins and doctors curing diseases for coins. I even saw two criminals murder a man just to get their hands on a few coins."

"Great Ba'al and Tanit!" cried Saponiba'al.

"Yes," said Wen-Amun, "that was terrible. But it made me realize something very important: Even though I myself didn't care about the coins, if I had some, I could buy anything I wanted! I could buy textiles from the Indian merchants, spices from the Arabs, perfume from the Greeks, and rotten fish sauce from the Carthaginians. And ever since realizing that, I've tried to get as many coins as I can."

"So," concluded Saponiba'al, **"in order to use money, I don't really need to believe in it at all. I just need to believe that other people believe in it!"**

What Saponiba'al understood is the big secret of money. That's how money can connect even foreigners who don't speak the same language and don't believe in the same gods. When you see that other people want money, you want it too. You can't actually do anything with money yourself. But if you have some, you can get other people to give you things or do things for you. What money is really made of isn't gold or paper or cowrie shells or electronic information. Money is made of trust. As long as you trust that other people want money, you trust the money too.

And what would happen if people ever lost their trust in money? What if farmers refused to sell figs for money, shoemakers refused to sell shoes for money, and barbers refused to cut hair for money? Then money would lose all its value and disappear.

Maybe you'll wake up tomorrow morning and people will no longer trust money, and then all the money you saved up over your life won't be worth anything. You might have a mountain of gold coins, but it couldn't buy a pair of shoes, or the computer will say you have a billion dollars, but all those dollars couldn't buy a single fig.

THE DANGERS OF MONEY

Money helped foreigners in the Carthage market to trust one another and cooperate. Today money helps people all over the world cooperate as well. Thanks to money, people on the other side of the world who don't know you and don't speak your language are nevertheless willing to grow food for you, write books for you, act in movies for you, and invent new medicines for you. Thanks to money, two people from anywhere in the world can cooperate. They don't need to believe in the same story about gods or dragons—they just need to believe that other people believe in money.

But money can also be extremely dangerous. In the Carthage market, people sometimes told the story of King Midas, who loved money more than anything else. He was king of the country of Phrygia, near Ephesus. One day King Midas met a sorcerer who said he could give the king whatever he wanted most in the world. King Midas thought about it for a while and said, "I want so many different things, it's hard to pick just one. I'll tell you what, give me the power to turn anything I touch into gold. That way, I can mint as many gold coins as I want and buy everything my heart desires." The sorcerer laughed and said, "Your wish is granted, King Midas. You now have the golden touch."

Midas decided to try his new power immediately. He picked up a small stone, and the moment he touched it, the stone became gold. He then touched a huge tree, and the entire tree turned into solid gold. The king was overjoyed and commanded his servants to cut down the gold tree, take it to the royal mint, and make a million gold coins out of it.

"**I've made enough money for one morning,**" he said contentedly. "Let's go back to the palace for lunch." He went to mount his favorite horse, but as he touched him, the horse turned into gold. Midas was a bit surprised. "What a pity!" he exclaimed. "He was my favorite horse. But it doesn't matter. I can buy all the horses in the world now!"

The king walked back to the palace and asked for his lunch. He was very hungry after all that money-making and walking, so while the cooks were preparing lunch, he grabbed an apple from one of the tables. As Midas brought the apple to his mouth, it turned to gold, and when he tried to bite it, he broke a tooth.

"Oh no!" cried Midas. "What will become of me? If I can't eat, I'll die of hunger!" He called the royal physician to concoct some medicine for him, but the king accidentally touched the physician, and he turned into a gold statue.

In horror, King Midas screamed so loudly that the queen rushed to see what was happening. Midas hugged her and cried on her shoulder, telling her everything that

happened . . . until he noticed she was cold and totally silent. **Midas had just turned his beloved wife into a lifeless lump of gold.**

Now everybody in the palace was terrified and ran from Midas as fast as their legs would carry them. The servants, the soldiers, and even the king's own children fled the palace for fear that Midas might touch them. The king himself went mad and threw himself out of the palace window into the river below. The moment he touched the water, it turned to solid gold, and the king died on impact with its hard shiny surface. Only then was his kingdom saved from the terror of his golden touch.

The story of King Midas is just a legend. No sorcerer can actually give you the power to turn everything into gold. But this legend has a very important message: It tells us that if we want to turn everything into money and then expect to buy whatever we want with our money, it will make us miserable and could destroy the whole world. **You can't buy friends or love for money, right?**

Money helps people cooperate even if they speak different languages and believe in different gods, but if we learn to trust only coins and banknotes, our hearts become as hard as solid gold, as if King Midas had touched them. We might see a poor man starving and not give him any food because he can't pay. We might see another poor woman shivering from cold and not give her any clothes because she has no money. Or we might see a

little girl sick with disease and not give her any medicine because she has no coins in her purse.

When money hardens people's hearts and makes them greedy, they can do even worse things. Criminals might rob and kill people just for money. Entire countries might go to war, just to make themselves richer. This is something the ancient Carthaginians understood well. Money helped make Carthage the biggest and richest city in the world, but the riches of Carthage's market attracted foreign enemies as well as foreign traders. The market that served as a meeting place for foreigners eventually became a battleground. Hanniba'al was right to be worried about the Romans because one day the wolf-people came to Carthage with a mighty army . . . and they weren't there to buy shoes for the legionnaires.

3
THE CHILDREN OF
THE BAD GUYS

LEARNING FROM
ENEMIES

HISTORY BOOKS ARE FULL OF WARS. SO ARE FANTASY BOOKS about sorcerers who fight with magic potions and secret spells. Games are also full of wars. Some kids spend many hours a week playing war games. Maybe you play a video game set in ancient times where you're a warrior traveling through various kingdoms and fighting other warriors with swords. In another video game, you might fly between stars and galaxies in a spaceship, battling aliens with laser guns.

Long before people invented computers, kids played at war using plastic guns, wooden swords, or toy soldiers. Over a thousand years ago, people in India invented chess, in which two armies fight each other until one king dies. The game was later adopted by the Persians, and the English word "checkmate" comes from the Persian term "shah mat," which means "the king is dead."

In real life too, wars have been common throughout history. **But wars weren't just about fighting and killing**—every war was also a meeting. During a war, people from different countries met, just like at the market, and this changed them in many ways. People saw what weapons their enemies used and started making similar weapons. People also saw what food their enemies ate, what clothes they wore, what games they played, and what gods they worshipped, and they occasionally adopted these things too. Sometimes people learned the most important things from their worst enemies.

The warring armies in a chess game never learn anything from each other. They just fight until one side manages to kill the opposing king, and then the game ends. When you play a video game where you shoot aliens, you don't learn anything from the aliens, and they don't learn from you. You just try to kill as many as you can before they kill you. Have you ever wondered what happens to the aliens in the video game after the fight's over, or what happens to the chess pawns on the losing side after their king dies?

To understand what happens in real life when different countries fight one another, let's go back to ancient Carthage and see what happened when the Roman legions arrived.

THE EMPIRE IS
COMING

Carthage was used to wars. The Carthaginians built a harbor and a market to welcome foreign traders, but they also built a wall all around their city. They used gold and silver to mint coins, but they also used iron to cast swords. Carthage attracted merchants from faraway cities and countries, but it also attracted many enemies.

The Romans were the worst enemies of Carthage. You may have heard of the Romans long before you read this book because they built one of the biggest empires in history—the Roman Empire. What exactly is this thing called an "empire" that the Romans built? **An empire is when one people conquers many foreign peoples and forces them to obey its commands.** The Romans conquered hundreds of foreign peoples and forced all of them to follow Roman orders and pay lots of taxes to Rome. Once they were part of the Roman Empire, all these hundreds of foreign people started speaking the Roman language, Latin. That's how Latin became so important and why even today countries use it to write things on their money and to name everything from viruses to humans. In Latin, "virus" means poison,

and the scientific name for humans, "homo," is just the Latin word for humans.

There were many empires in history besides the Roman Empire: There was a Chinese Empire, an Arab Empire, a Spanish Empire, and a British Empire. That's why so many people in the world now speak Chinese, Arabic, Spanish, and English—English is the language of the British Empire. No matter who you are, some of your ancestors probably lived under one of these empires.

The Romans wanted to add Carthage to their empire too, and they fought several wars with the Carthaginians. In the biggest of these wars, the Carthaginian general Hanniba'al won many battles and took his army and his war elephants all the way to the gates of Rome . . . but the Romans eventually defeated him. Then it was the Roman army's turn to get closer and closer to the gates of Carthage.

Now that it had defeated Hanniba'al, Rome was much stronger than Carthage, but Carthage was still a big and rich city, and it still had lots of soldiers and weapons. It had tens of thousands of strong iron swords, dozens of powerful warships, and about 2,000 big war machines called

catapults. These catapults were made of iron and wood and could throw large stones for hundreds of yards, smashing entire houses and ships.

The Romans knew it would be difficult to conquer Carthage by force alone. So they decided to use a trick: They offered to make peace with Carthage on the condition that the Carthaginians first gave up all their weapons. "If we have peace, what do you need all your weapons for?" said the Romans.

The Carthaginians were suspicious. They weren't sure if they could trust the Romans. On the other hand, they were tired of war, and they knew Rome was now stronger than them. So they accepted the Roman peace offer. They collected all their swords, warships, and catapults, and either destroyed them or gave them to the Romans.

After the last sword was handed over, the last catapult smashed, and the last warship burned, the Romans said, "Oh, we forgot to tell you we have another condition: **We'll make peace with you only if you abandon your city of Carthage** and move someplace else. We'll burn your city to the ground and *then* you can have peace."

The Carthaginians were appalled. They loved their

city, which had been their home for hundreds of years. They loved the streets where neighbors met and gossiped, the squares where they played as kids, the temples of Ba'al and Tanit where they prayed to the gods, the beaches where they collected seashells, and the colorful market where they bought shoes and rotten fish sauce. They didn't want to abandon it all.

Besides, they now knew the Romans were liars. Even if the Carthaginians agreed to abandon Carthage, how could they trust the Romans to make peace? Maybe the Romans were lying again, and after burning Carthage, they would enslave all the Carthaginians? The Carthaginians didn't want to be slaves, so—even though they now had no swords, catapults, or warships—they decided to stay in their city and fight.

People brought pots and pans from their kitchens and melted them down to make swords. They dismantled their chairs, tables, beds, and doors and used the wood to make new catapults. They even broke down entire houses and used the long, strong beams to build new ships.

To build ships and catapults, the Carthaginians needed not just wood but also flexible rope, but where could they get enough rope? They didn't have time to sail to distant lands to buy it. So any Carthaginian man, woman, or child with long hair cut their hair to make ropes with it! Being bald was suddenly very fashionable, even for women and girls like Batba'al and Saponiba'al. Everybody who knew how to swing a sword, hoist a sail, or hold an oar—like Saponiba'al's brother Hanniba'al—joined the army or the navy. The Carthaginians were determined to save their beloved city and teach the Roman bullies a lesson.

What do you think happened then? It turned out the Romans were just too strong for them. **The huge Roman army commanded by General Scipio defeated the brave Carthaginians.** Scipio's soldiers breached the walls of Carthage and poured into the city like a torrent of water breaking through a dam. For six days the Romans went from street to street, killing everybody they saw and burning all the houses. Modern archaeologists have found many remains from this terrible attack, like houses burned to the ground, big round stones thrown by catapults, lots

of arrowheads, and human skeletons buried under the rubble.

Eventually, Scipio ordered his soldiers to stop killing the Carthaginians. Instead, they enslaved about 50,000 people who had survived in the city, shipped them to Rome and other places, and sold them for a few gold coins. A girl like Saponiba'al, who was once happy and free in her village, ended up enslaved by a rich Roman family.

The Romans allowed other Carthaginians to go on living in the small towns and villages near Carthage. Perhaps Saponiba'al's brother Hanniba'al returned to their village, and Batba'al joined him there. They were very sad about what happened to Saponiba'al and the destruction of Carthage, but they hoped that one day things would get better. In the meantime, life in the village was difficult. Scipio allowed the villagers to live there but only if they paid very high taxes to Rome and never tried to rebuild the city of Carthage, which was now a heap of ruins. The great city that had once been home to hundreds of thousands of people was now home to no one except spiders, scorpions, and lizards.

You might find this ending disappointing. **We're used to stories with happy endings**, in which the bullies and liars lose. We come across stories like these in books and movies all the time. The bad guys seem very powerful, they lie and cheat and do lots of unfair things, but then along comes a hero like Spider-Man or Wonder Woman,

and against all odds, the good guys win. Sure, in most action movies the good guys lose at first. It would be boring if they won from the start. If Spider-Man defeated the bad guys in the first five minutes, it wouldn't be much of a movie. So usually the bad guys trick Spider-Man, and maybe even capture him and put him in the most secure prison ever invented . . . but then Spider-Man finds a way out or Wonder Woman comes to help him, and at the very last moment they defeat the bad guys. It's almost always like that in the movies. Unfortunately, in real life it's not like that. **The bad guys sometimes win.**

GLADIATOR
SCHOOL

The Romans defeated not just the Carthaginians but also the Greeks, the Jews, the Egyptians, the Britons, and hundreds of other peoples. They burned down many other cities besides Carthage, enslaved numerous people, and forced everyone to serve the Romans. This is how they built the Roman Empire. People in many lands could tell terrible stories about the Romans—but they had to do it quietly so the Romans wouldn't hear them and punish them.

If the enslaved Carthaginian girl Saponiba'al met other enslaved children, they could have whispered dreadful stories to each other.

"When the Romans destroyed Carthage," said Saponiba'al, "they enslaved me and sent me to Rome, where a rich Roman bought me at the market for a hundred gold coins. I have to do everything he says. I wake up every day long before sunrise to make breakfast for his family. If I'm lucky, they let me eat the leftovers. Then I have to wash the dishes, clean the floor, launder their clothes, and go to the well for water. All day I'm just running, washing, and cleaning. If they see me take a rest without their permission, they beat me. Long after sunset, when they're already snoring in their beds, I have to prepare clean clothes for them to wear the next day. When I can finally go to sleep, I have to sleep on the floor in my

dirty clothes, next to the big, smelly family dog. And they don't pay me a single gold coin for all the work I do, because I am their slave."

"I was captured and enslaved by the Romans too," said a Jewish boy. "They forced me to work in a gold mine. I have to go down into the mine every morning. It's a tunnel dug deep under a huge mountain. There's no light in there and hardly any air. I dig all day, looking for gold. When I come out in the evening, the sun's already gone down. The Romans give me moldy bread to eat, and they take all the gold I find. They mint coins with the gold, but they never give any of them to me. They get very rich doing nothing, while I work hard all day and I'm still very poor."

Then a Greek boy told them how the Romans burned his city, took him from his parents, and sold him to a gladiator school. "These Romans love to watch gladiator fights, but they don't want to risk their own lives, so they capture foreigners to be their gladiators! In gladiator school we learn how to fight with a sword or a spear. Then they take us to the big arena and make us fight lions or bears. It's so scary. I just have a little sword in my hand to fight big ferocious animals, while the Romans sit in the audience, shouting and eating and laughing. A month ago, one of my best friends was killed by a bear, and the Romans just laughed about it! But the worst thing is when they force us to fight our own friends from gladiator school. And if two friends refuse to fight each other, the Romans just kill both of them."

IT'S OKAY WHEN
WE DO IT

If you're like most humans, you probably think that empires are very unfair. Would you like to take orders from a bunch of foreigners who force you to wash their smelly underwear or fight your friends? We humans love our freedom. **Even if one group of people is very strong and powerful, it's totally unfair for them to bully weaker peoples**, destroy their cities, and turn them into slaves.

So most humans agree that empires are unfair, but there's one exception to this rule. Whenever a nation becomes very strong and manages to conquer an empire, a lot of people in that nation think *their* empire is perfectly okay. It's bad when foreigners tell us what to do, but it's great when we tell them what to do. That's like a kid in school who hates being beaten by bullies but thinks it's fine for him to beat other kids and be a bully himself.

The Carthaginians, for example, hated the Roman Empire and didn't like doing what the Romans commanded. But **before they were conquered by the Romans, the Carthaginians had an empire of their own** and behaved cruelly to many other peoples. The land on which the Phoenician settlers built the city of Carthage had previously belonged to local Numidian tribes. You remember the legend about Queen Elissa, who won the

land by cleverly tricking a local king, Iarbas? That was just a made-up story; in truth, the Phoenician settlers probably took the land by force.

The Carthaginians then conquered many other nearby lands that belonged to various North African peoples. They also conquered more distant islands like Sicily, Sardinia, and Corsica, and their famous general Hanniba'al even conquered parts of Spain. Hanniba'al and other Carthaginian generals destroyed many cities and enslaved many people, just like the Romans eventually destroyed Carthage and enslaved its people.

The Greeks also had an empire before the Romans conquered them. The Greek leader Alexander the Great fought many wars, destroyed many cities, and built an empire that stretched all the way from Greece to India. It was in India that the Greeks saw people using war elephants. They copied the idea and then spread it to the Carthaginians and Romans.

Even the Jews had an empire, or at least this is what they liked to believe. They proudly told a story that when they first came to the land of Canaan, the place was full

of many other peoples like the Canaanites and Amorites, but the Jews conquered them, killed many, enslaved others, and burned or took their cities. The Jews were particularly proud of taking the famous city of Jerusalem. They said that King David, the greatest of all Jewish kings, conquered Jerusalem, killed or enslaved its inhabitants, and made Jerusalem the capital of a Jewish Empire. Later, the Romans came and took Jerusalem from the Jews, killing and enslaving many of them. Then the Jews complained about the Romans' cruelty, saying it was very unfair of the Romans to behave like that. But the Jews also raised their spirits by telling stories about how wonderful things were in the old days of the Jewish Empire.

"Ah," they would tell one another, "we too once had an empire! The great King David won lots of wars, and burned other people's cities, and turned those people into our slaves. Let's pray that one day a new king like David will come, and we'll win wars and have an empire again!"

Some wise Jews said that maybe this was the wrong prayer, and they should actually pray that there wouldn't be any wars or empires at all—neither a Roman Empire nor a Jewish one. These wise Jews said, "If you don't like being conquered and enslaved, why do you want to do it to other people?" Wise people in Greece, India, China, and almost everywhere else in the world had the same idea. And it's simple enough: **Don't do to others what you don't like others to do to you.**

This idea may sound obvious, but for thousands of years most people in the world weren't very wise and didn't agree with it. They cried bitterly if anyone tried to conquer them but were very proud whenever they succeeded in conquering others. Only in recent generations have most people in the world started accepting that *all* empires are bad, and if we manage to conquer other people, it isn't something to be proud of. If our own people are very strong and manage to build an empire, this still isn't fair, and we shouldn't do it. It's not only other people's empires that are bad. Our empire is bad too.

BECOMING ROMANS

But history is very complicated. Many of the people conquered by empires eventually came to like these empires. For example, after the Roman Empire conquered Carthage, many Carthaginians began to think that the Roman Empire was a good thing, and even began to call themselves "Romans."

How can that be? If a bully at school beats you up, steals your things, and makes you miserable one day, would you start to like that bully the next day? Obviously not. However, given enough time, strange things can happen. Time is like a powerful magician that can change almost

everything. Time can turn love into hate and hate into love. Time can make people forget their most important memories and remember things that never happened at all. **Given enough time, people can forget their language, their gods, and their games and adopt the language, the gods, and the games of the empire that conquered them instead.** This is what happened to the Carthaginians.

After Scipio destroyed Carthage, the city remained a heap of ruins inhabited by spiders and scorpions for a hundred years. Then another Roman general called Julius Caesar decided to rebuild it. He gave orders to clear the ruins, build houses and temples, and open a harbor. The scorpions and spiders had to move out, while poor Romans who had no land in Rome came and moved in. Caesar also allowed the Carthaginians who lived in the nearby towns and villages to come back to the new Carthage. Perhaps one of Hanniba'al and Batba'al's grandchildren did exactly that.

Julius Caesar was murdered, and his great-nephew Augustus became the empire's new ruler—now called "the emperor." Augustus continued to rebuild Carthage, and Romans and Carthaginians became neighbors in the new city. They walked the same streets, went to the same shops, and even prayed in the same temples. Their children sometimes played together in the squares and collected seashells on the sandy beaches. Every now and then a Roman girl and a Carthaginian boy fell in love, and perhaps got married and had children. Carthage grew

and prospered, and within another hundred years, it was one of the biggest cities in the world again. **It was also now hard to tell who was Carthaginian and who was Roman.** Many people had one grandparent from Carthage and another from Rome.

The Carthaginians learned to speak the Roman language, Latin. It was much more useful than Phoenician, because people from all over the empire spoke Latin. Nowadays if you speak English, you can talk not just with English people, but also with Canadians, Greeks, Brazilians, and Nigerians. Similarly, in the Roman Empire, if you spoke Latin, you could talk not just with Romans but with numerous other people.

The Carthaginians even became fond of some Roman games. They didn't like gladiator fights very much, but they came to love theater. In Rome, theater was a big thing, so when the Romans rebuilt Carthage, they constructed a theater there too and brought actors from Rome to perform all the best plays. Both Romans and Carthaginians flocked to watch these plays. They watched tragedies together and cried when children were separated from their mothers. They watched dramas together and applauded when the good guys defeated the bad guys. They watched comedies together and laughed loudly when somebody farted on stage.

While the Carthaginians were becoming more like Romans, the Romans were also learning many things from all the people they conquered. One thing the Romans got from conquered people was theater. Wait,

didn't we just say the Romans loved theater and brought it to Carthage? Yes, but theater didn't originate in Rome. The Romans were good at fighting, not at acting. It was the Greeks who invented theater. But when the Romans conquered Greek cities, like Athens and Ephesus, they saw how much fun the Greeks had with their theaters, so they built a theater in Rome. They brought Greek actors to perform in Rome, and even brought Greek writers to write new plays. People in Rome used to joke that after Rome conquered the Greeks with the sword, the Greeks conquered Rome with theater!

As theater became popular in the Roman Empire and spread to places like Carthage, not only Greeks and Romans acted on stage and wrote plays. One of the best playwrights of the Roman Empire came from Carthage. We don't know his original name, but we do know that his mother was a

slave. When he was a boy, he was sold to a rich Roman called Terentius Lucanus and was known as "the slave of Terentius Lucanus"—or Terence for short.

Terence was such an intelligent boy and he learned Latin so well that his master Terentius Lucanus freed him. As a teenager, Terence was already fascinated by theater. **Perhaps he loved it because even a slave can be king for an hour onstage.** Terence began writing plays that were staged in Rome and other cities. Many of his most successful plays had something in common: The main character was a poor or enslaved child who discovered they actually came from a rich and powerful family. For example, in the play *The Girl from Andros*, a poor girl named Glycerium turns out to be the daughter of a rich Athenian nobleman! Glycerium was separated from her father as a child and only discovered her true identity when she grew up. It's hardly surprising that Terence, a Carthaginian slave, loved inventing stories about poor kids discovering they're the children of powerful, wealthy people.

Nor is it surprising that many other people loved hearing these stories. Terence's plays were staged again and again for hundreds of years, and schoolchildren who learned Latin often did so by reading his plays because his Latin was just perfect. Even today lots of people dream their lives will turn out like a Terence play, and they'll suddenly discover they're the lost child of some billionaire or king. So theaters still stage the plays written by that ancient Carthaginian slave, and people still admire his style.

EVERYBODY
IS ROMAN

Terence wasn't the only Carthaginian who made it big in Rome. About 350 years after the Romans destroyed Carthage, a **Carthaginian called Septimius Severus did something that would have utterly amazed Hanniba'al, Batba'al, and Saponiba'al—and amazed the Romans too**. Let's eavesdrop on a conversation between two imaginary Roman girls to find out what it was.

"Have you heard the news?" asked one Roman girl, called Cassia.

"No," said her friend Herodias. "What happened?"

"A Carthaginian has just become emperor of Rome!"

"What?!" cried Herodias. "How is that possible?"

"Well," explained Cassia, "when the last emperor was murdered, the army generals began fighting among themselves about who would be the next emperor. I've just heard that Septimius Severus won, and he's now emperor."

"Where did this Septimius guy come from?" asked Herodias.

"His mother is from a Roman family," said Cassia.

"Ah, so he *is* Roman after all! But didn't you say he was Carthaginian?"

"You should let me finish my sentences! His mother is Roman, but his father's family is Carthaginian. I've heard Septimius spoke Phoenician at home and only learned

Latin at school! Then he joined the Roman army and rose to become a general."

"You don't say!" gasped Herodias. "So this Carthaginian became a Roman general, just like Scipio and Caesar, and now he's our emperor . . . Great Jupiter and Mars, how things change!"

This really was a surprising turnaround. It's as if the black army in a game of chess defeated the white army and killed the white king, but then a white pawn somehow worked its way to the top and became the new black king.

Several years later, Cassia and Herodias met again, and this time it was Herodias who amazed Cassia.

"Have you heard the news?" asked Herodias.

"No," said Cassia. "What happened?"

"Well, you know that after Septimius Severus died, his son Caracalla was made emperor and—"

"Everyone knows that!" interrupted Cassia. "That was a whole year ago! That's not news."

"Sure," agreed Herodias, "but you should let me finish my sentences! Because I bet you don't know what Caracalla did just now! He gave Roman citizenship to everyone in the empire! Well, except

for slaves, of course. That means every free person in the Roman Empire is now a Roman!"

Cassia was stunned. "You mean the Greeks are now Romans and the Jews are now Romans?"

"Exactly," said Herodias, "and the Carthaginians are now Romans too."

"This is so confusing," said Cassia. "Great Jupiter and Mars, how things change!"

THE BOY WHO BECAME EMPEROR

Many people in the Roman Empire were very happy that Emperor Caracalla made all of them Romans. But there was one person who didn't like Caracalla very much—the commander of Caracalla's own bodyguard, a man called Macrinus. **According to some ancient historians, Macrinus wanted to become emperor himself.** "Why should I earn just a few gold coins from Caracalla to protect his life," thought Macrinus, "when I can kill him, become emperor, and then have all the gold in the empire to myself?"

One day, Macrinus had Caracalla killed. Caracalla was traveling and wanted to go to the toilet. He went behind a bush and took down his underwear, and Macrinus sent someone to surprise the emperor and stab him. Macrinus

then became emperor and got all the gold of the empire. But he also got a lot of things to worry about. He knew there were plenty of people who now wanted to get rid of him and make themselves emperor. He was constantly terrified some general or bodyguard would murder him—perhaps when he went to the toilet—and he didn't know whether hiring more bodyguards would protect him or put him in more danger. "I could pay as many bodyguards as I want," he thought, "but who would protect me from all the bodyguards?!"

So it must have come as a huge surprise to Macrinus when he lost the empire not to a general or a bodyguard, but to a fourteen-year-old boy called Varius. This boy lived in the small town of Emesa in Phoenicia, the same region from which the first settlers of Carthage came. The news must have stunned not just Macrinus but anyone who heard about it.

"Have you heard the news?" cried Cassia at the top of her voice.

"Oh, what now?" sighed Herodias.

"We have a new emperor—a fourteen-year-old boy from Phoenicia!"

"What?" said Herodias. "Another new emperor? But how is that possible? I thought Macrinus was emperor. It hasn't even been a year since he killed Caracalla. And now he's lost the empire to a fourteen-year-old boy? You must be kidding!"

"This boy Varius," explained Cassia, "started telling people that he's Caracalla's lost son, so he should be

emperor, not Macrinus. Actually I've heard it wasn't even Varius himself who came up with that story, but his grandmother Julia Maesa. She probably really wanted her grandson to be emperor."

"Is it true?" asked Herodias. "Is Varius really Caracalla's son?"

"How should I know?" replied Cassia. "But apparently lots of people *believe* Varius really is Caracalla's son."

"It might be true," mused Herodias. "Last week I saw this play by Terence about a poor boy who suddenly discovered his father was some bigshot. If it can happen onstage, why can't it happen in real life too?"

"Anyhow," continued Cassia, "when Macrinus heard about all this, he sent soldiers to kill Julia Maesa and Varius. But lots of the soldiers started believing the boy's story."

"Maybe," said Herodias, "the soldiers loved theater and loved a good story about lost children discovering their true parents?"

"Maybe," agreed Cassia. "Anyway, there was a big battle. The soldiers who supported Varius defeated the soldiers who supported Macrinus. Then they killed Macrinus and made Varius the new emperor."

"And you say this Varius boy is Phoenician?"

"He *comes* from somewhere in that region," explained Cassia. "But some people say he's half Arab. Does it matter? The Arabs are also Romans."

"Great Jupiter and Mars!" said Herodias. "How things change!"

THE EMPEROR'S
NEW WEDDING

Now not only was everybody Roman but almost anybody could be emperor of Rome, even a fourteen-year-old half-Arab boy from Phoenicia. **But Varius soon found out that being emperor wasn't all sunshine.** His grandmother Julia Maesa constantly nagged him to sit quietly and listen to long speeches from politicians, answer letters from governors, and carefully calculate which taxes people should pay and how much money to give the soldiers and bodyguards. She thought that's what emperors should do. The boy had other ideas. "What's the point of being the most powerful person in the world," thought Varius, "if you don't get to have any fun?"

"Have you heard the news?" Herodias called out to Cassia.

"Yes, I have!" Cassia smiled. "I heard Emperor Varius stopped going to the Senate to hear politicians give long speeches. He spends his time driving in chariot races instead! And organizing the most extravagant parties he can think of!"

"Well," said Herodias. "I've heard he's getting married."

"Again?!" said Cassia. "That boy sure loves weddings. How many did he have already?"

"Well"—Herodias counted on her fingers—"first he married Julia Cornelia Paula. Then he divorced her and married Julia Aquilia. Then he divorced her and married Annia Aurelia. Then he divorced Annia and married Julia Aquilia again."

"So does that count as four wives," wondered Cassia, "or three?"

"And don't forget the husbands!" said Herodias.

"Oh, I remember!" Cassia said with a grin. "It was the talk of the town for a whole month! They said Emperor Varius went to a chariot race, and this charioteer called Hierocles crashed his chariot and fell right in front of the emperor's seat. When Hierocles's helmet rolled off his head, the emperor was so struck by his beautiful blond hair that he fell in love with him on the spot. They got married soon after."

"But then he dumped him," added Herodias, "and married that Greek athlete Zoticus from that town near Ephesus."

"No," Cassia disagreed, "I think he's still married to Hierocles too. And to Julia Aquilia, of course. **And to think this multi-marrying emperor is only eighteen!** Actually I heard he no longer wants to be called emperor. He wants to be called empress instead."

"What?" Herodias asked in disbelief.

"When someone saluted him recently and said, 'My Lord Emperor!' Varius snapped, 'Don't call me lord. I am a lady.'"

"Great Jupiter and Mars!" concluded Herodias. "How things change!"

So Varius spent his time on chariot races, parties, and weddings, instead of listening to boring speeches and reading boring letters as his grandmother said he should. Julia Maesa was very upset with Varius and thought she picked the wrong grandson to be emperor. She then paid the body-

guards lots of money to get rid of Varius and told people that another one of her grandkids—a boy called Alexander—was also a lost son of Caracalla. So they made Alexander the new emperor. Alexander was about thirteen at the time, and unlike Varius, he always did exactly what his grandmother told him. Alexander knew that nobody could mess with Julia Maesa—not even the emperor of Rome.

A NEW GOD

When Julia Maesa and her grandsons came to Rome from Emesa to rule the empire, they brought something with them—a god called Elagabal. Elagabal was the chief god of Emesa, where people said he was the god of the sun. There was a big temple to him in the middle of the town, and in that temple was a black stone that people said came from the sky. Maybe the stone was a meteorite that really did come from the sky. The boy-emperor Varius brought the black stone to Rome with him, built a new temple in Rome for the sun god Elagabal, and told the Romans many stories about the god. He even minted new coins with an image of the sacred black stone on them. **Most Romans had never heard of Elagabal, but new gods were a common thing in the empire.** When people moved around the empire, they often brought

their gods with them to new places.

Back in the days of Scipio, the Romans believed in the gods Jupiter, Mars, and Venus; the Greeks believed in Artemis, Zeus, and Athena; the Carthaginians believed in Ba'al, Tanit, and many other gods like the god of medicine Eshmun; and the rest of the tribes and peoples in the empire each had their own gods. But as they came together under one empire, talking with one another, going to see the same plays, and sometimes even getting married, **people began to mix their gods**.

If they heard about some particularly interesting god worshipped by another people, they might go and visit that god's temple. Lots of people went to Ephesus to visit the famous temple of Artemis. When a Roman was sick, he might go to the temple of the Carthaginian healing god Eshmun and pray for Eshmun to cure him. When a Carthaginian girl fell in love with a Roman boy, she might go to the temple of the Roman love goddess Venus and ask her to make sure the boy loves her back. Maybe Venus couldn't do this, and maybe Venus didn't exist at all, but when you're in love, you'll do almost anything. It may not help, but it won't do any harm.

Just as the god Elagabal moved from Phoenicia to Rome, many other stories about gods circulated around

the empire. Even before Elagabal came to Rome, people in the empire had started hearing a particularly interesting and important story from a land just to the south of Phoenicia. The first to tell this story were some Jews. Previously, Jews like Jonah the sailor believed in a big god who sat high in the sky and ruled the whole world. They had many names for him—Yahweh, Ya, Elohim, Adonai, and more, and sometimes they just called him "the god" or "the father." Later other people gave this god even more names. All these names caused a lot of confusion, so to keep things simple, we'll follow Jonah the sailor and call him the Sky Father.

The Jews said that the Sky Father created the entire world and all the people in it. They also said their god was so powerful he could do anything he wanted—like make the sun disappear or part the sea. But there was something that didn't sound right about these stories. If the Jewish god was so powerful, why did he let the Romans conquer the Jews and make many of them slaves? The Jews thought about this for a long, long time but couldn't find an answer.

Then some of the Jews began telling a new story: They said the Sky Father had sent a man called Jesus to explain everything. Jesus grew up in the small village of Nazareth, where the locals knew him as the son of a poor carpenter. But his followers were convinced he was actually the son of the Sky Father—a bit like in one of Terence's plays, when a poor boy turns out to be the son of someone very

powerful. Jesus's followers also said that he proved he really was the son of the Sky Father by performing amazing miracles, making the blind see and the deaf hear and even bringing dead people back to life.

Jesus also told people that what happened here on Earth didn't really matter: It was all like one of those plays everybody loved. In a play, you can be many different things, but when the play ends, it doesn't matter what you were, right? **Maybe onstage you were the emperor and everybody obeyed you.** But if you tried to order the other actors to wash your dirty clothes once the play was

finished, they would laugh at you and say, "The show's over, dummy. We're not *really* your slaves. You want your clothes washed? Do it yourself!"

Jesus said that life is like a play that ends when we die. And when we die, it doesn't matter whether we were an emperor or a slave during our lifetime. That's why the Sky Father allowed the Romans to conquer and enslave the Jews, the Carthaginians, and the Greeks. It was all just theater.

After all, people live on Earth for just a few decades. Even if you're the emperor of Rome, you die in the end, and your body's eaten by maggots.

But, Jesus said, if you believe in the Sky Father, then when you die the Sky Father takes you to a wonderful place called heaven, where you can enjoy eternal bliss, even if you were just a slave here on Earth. If you don't believe what Jesus said, then you're sent to a terrible place called hell when you die, and demons roast you in fire for millions of years, even if you were emperor of Rome on Earth. And heaven and hell aren't theater: They last forever—the show's never over. That's how Jesus explained it all.

Some Jews didn't believe a word Jesus said. "You aren't the son of the Sky Father!" they said. "You're just the son of a poor carpenter from Nazareth!" Other Jews did believe Jesus, and called him "Christ," which in the Greek language means "someone smeared with oil." What has oil got to do with it? Well, the ancient Jews believed that when the Sky Father sends someone to represent him on Earth, that person is smeared with very special sky oil in a ceremony called "anointing." Those who thought Jesus really came from the Sky Father claimed he had this sky oil, so they called him "the one anointed with oil" or "Christ." And they called themselves Christians—people who follow Christ, the anointed one.

The Christians told stories about Jesus Christ and the Sky Father and heaven and hell to many other people who weren't Jews. They told them to the people of Ephesus, and Thebes, and Carthage, and even to the people of Rome. "It doesn't matter if you're a slave or an emperor—you just need to believe in Jesus Christ, then when you die, the Sky Father will take you to heaven!"

The Christians couldn't prove that this story was true. **Nobody came back after they died to tell people they now lived in heaven or hell** or anywhere else. Nobody knew for sure what happened to people after they died. Life may be like a play, but nobody knows what happens when the curtain comes down.

Still, people often believe a story not because they have strong proof that it's true but because they have a

100

strong desire to believe it is. People who had difficult and poor lives desperately wanted to believe that when they died, they could go to this wonderful heaven. It sounded even better than discovering that your father was actually a millionaire or an emperor.

TOO MANY STORIES
ABOUT JESUS

There was a problem, though. As more and more people in the Roman Empire became Christians, they began telling different stories about Jesus and what he said. Whenever they wanted to convince people of something, they would say "Jesus said it!" and it became more and more difficult to know what Jesus had really said.

The Christian leaders held meetings about this, first in a town called Hippo near Carthage and then in the city of Carthage itself. Carthage was one of the most important centers for early Christians—perhaps because the Carthaginians liked the idea that it didn't matter who won wars on Earth, it was what happened after you died that mattered.

During their meeting in Carthage, the Christian leaders went over all the different stories that people told about the Sky Father and Jesus, chose the stories that they thought seemed true, and made a single book out of

these stories. They called this book "the Bible," and they forbade anyone to add any other stories to it or delete any stories from it. Even today billions of people all over the world own a copy of this Bible, which contains only the stories that were accepted in this meeting held in Carthage long ago. If the people at the meeting in Carthage made a mistake and put the wrong stories in the book, then everybody today is reading the wrong stories about the Sky Father and Jesus.

So the Christian religion started with the Jews, passed to other people like the inhabitants of Ephesus and Carthage, and then the Carthaginians helped convince even Roman emperors to become Christians. **Who really conquered whom?** Yes, the Romans first conquered the Greeks, the Jews, and the Carthaginians. But then the Greeks conquered Rome with their theater, and the Jews and the Carthaginians conquered Rome with their religions. To go back to the game of chess, it's as if the

black army defeated the white army and killed the white king, but then the black pawns and even the black king turned white, or perhaps all the pieces on the board—black and white alike—turned gray.

VANDALS
AND GHOSTS

Eventually, the Roman Empire fell. Exactly 600 years after Scipio burned Carthage, an army sailed from Carthage and conquered the city of Rome. But this wasn't a Carthaginian army, it was a Vandal army. The Vandals were a new people from the far north who invaded the Roman Empire, defeated the Roman army, took over Carthage, and used it as a base to attack the city of Rome itself. When the Vandals conquered Rome, they killed so many people, burned so many houses, and created such a big mess that the word "vandal" was later used for anyone who ruins things. If a kid in school throws garbage on the floor, tears a book, or draws graffiti on the walls, a teacher might shout "Stop vandalizing the place!"

The Carthaginians themselves weren't happy at all about how the Vandals vandalized Rome. **By now the Carthaginians thought of themselves as Romans and saw the Vandals as new conquerors rather than liberators.** Imagine a Carthaginian boy called Augustinus who

just heard that the Vandals conquered Rome—he would feel very sad about it. And imagine that he suddenly saw a very strange sight: a ghost laughing and jumping for joy.

"Who are you?" asked Augustinus in amazement. "I've never seen a ghost before. Certainly not a happy ghost that laughs and jumps for joy."

"I am the ghost of your ancestor, Hanniba'al. I was a Carthaginian soldier who fought against Scipio. I've waited six hundred years for revenge, and now finally I've heard the good news: Rome has fallen! Hooray! Happy day!"

"I heard the news too," said Augustinus, "but it made me very sad."

"But why are you so sad, my boy? This is a time for celebration! Why aren't you happy the Romans have been defeated?"

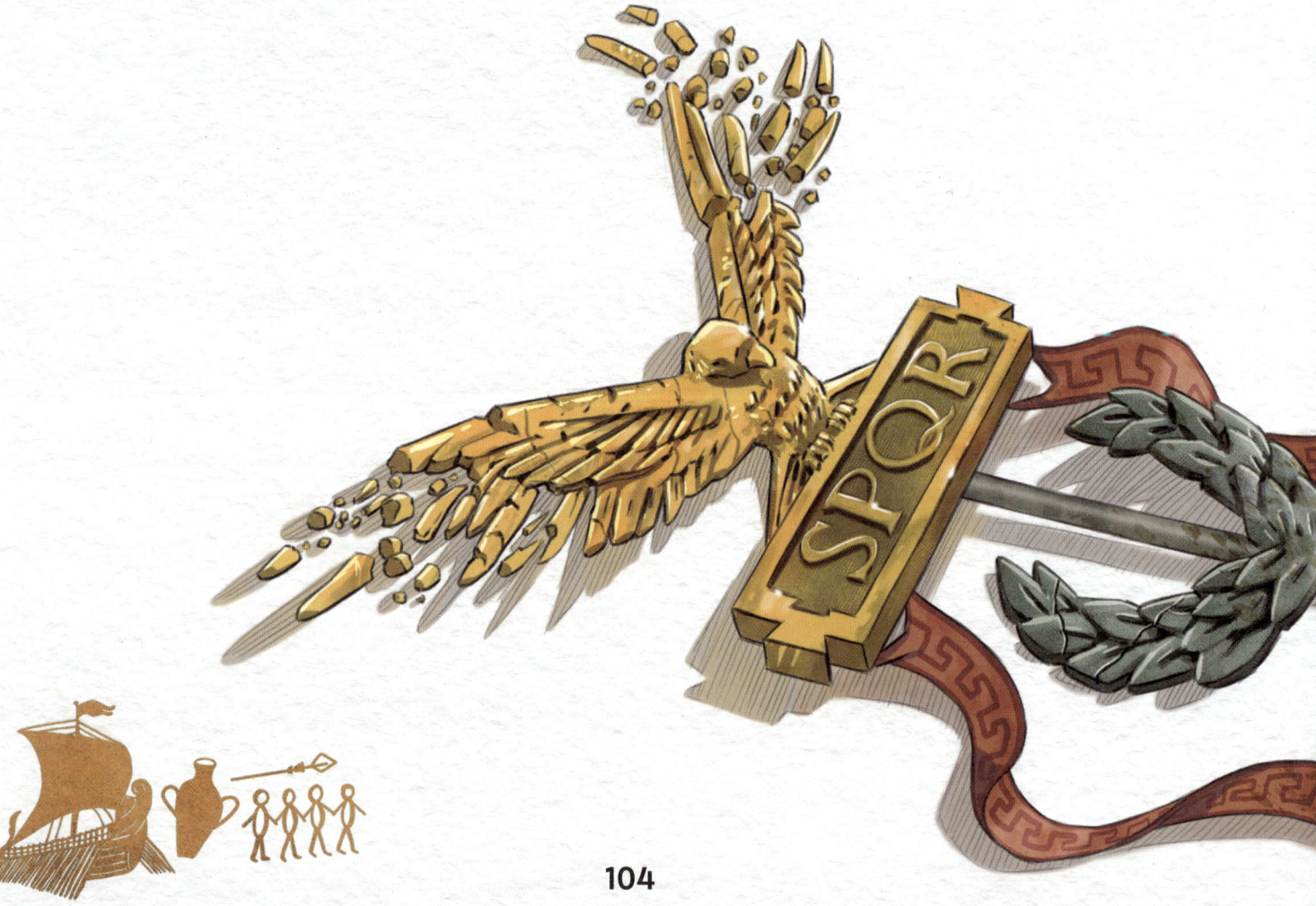

"I'm Roman myself. Why should I be happy about the Romans' defeat?"

"Great Ba'al and Tanit!" cried Hanniba'al's ghost. "You're not Roman! You're Carthaginian! The Romans are your enemies!"

"Yes, I'm Carthaginian, but Carthaginians are Romans. Can't you tell from my name—Augustinus? I'm named after the greatest of all Roman emperors, Augustus."

"Great Ba'al and Tanit!" cried the ghost. "Augustinus is no name for a good Carthaginian boy! How about changing your name to Hanniba'al?"

"Thanks, but I prefer Augustinus. All my friends in my Latin class call me Augi for short."

"Latin class?! You study the language of our enemies?!"

"Latin's our mother tongue," explained Augustinus. "We speak it at home too. But in Latin class we learn to read and write proper Latin. I came first in our Latin test last week! When I grow up, I want to be a playwright for the theater, just like my hero, Terence."

"Great Ba'al and Tanit! True Carthaginians don't like theater!"

"Who are these Ba'al and Tanit guys you keep talking about?" asked Augustinus.

"What? You don't know Ba'al and Tanit? You forgot the gods of your ancestors?! Which gods do you worship then?"

"Like all good Romans, I only worship one god—the Sky Father—and his son, Jesus Christ."

"But this is terrible!" shouted the ghost. "As your ancestor, I insist you change your name to Hanniba'al, go back to speaking Phoenician, go back to worshipping Ba'al and Tanit, and stop all this theater nonsense!"

"But I barely know how to speak Phoenician, and I like going to church to pray to Jesus, and I like theater, and I definitely don't want to change my name. Why should I do any of that?"

"Why? Because you're my descendant, and as my descendant, you should speak my language, worship my gods, and enjoy my art! Never could I imagine that a descendant of mine would consider himself a Roman!"

Then another, even older ghost appeared.

"Stop heckling the boy, Hanniba'al!" said the very old ghost.

"Who are you?" asked Hanniba'al in a ghostly voice.

"I am King Iarbas, the Numidian," said the very old ghost, "and I am *your* ancestor. I lived six hundred years before you, and I'm disappointed with you, Hanniba'al."

"Why's that?" Hanniba'al's ghost asked.

"You're my descendant and yet you adopted the name, language, and gods of my worst enemies, the Carthaginians! You see, six hundred years before you were born, my people lived in peace and prosperity, until suddenly these Phoenician invaders appeared from across the sea. They took our land, built their city of Carthage on it, and made us work for them. We hated them, but we couldn't resist them. They were too powerful. Still, never would I have imagined that a descendant of mine would see himself as Carthaginian! If the boy here calls himself by a Roman name and speaks Latin, that's a shame, but at least it's better than you calling yourself by a Carthaginian name and speaking Phoenician!"

Which of his ancestors do you think Augustinus should listen to—Hanniba'al or Iarbas?

Actually it's even more complicated than that. **People always have more than one ancestor.** You have two parents, right? Each of them also has two parents, so you have four grandparents. Each of your grandparents has two parents, so that makes eight great-grandparents. All of them had two parents each, so if you go back about

100 years, you would find you have 16 great-great-grandparents. Go back 200 years and you have 256 ancestors. Go back 300 years and it's 4,096 ancestors. Go back 600 years . . . and you have millions of ancestors!

So if the boy Augustinus could meet his ancestors who lived hundreds of years before his time, there wouldn't be just one or two ghosts. There would be a crowd of millions of ghosts. And these millions of ancestors came from many different places.

"We're from Carthage!" cried one group of ghosts. "And we insist that you, boy, should speak Phoenician!"

"We're Numidians!" shouted another group of ghosts. "We don't like Phoenicians at all. The boy should speak our language!"

"We're Romans," said some other ghosts, "and we think the boy's right. He should speak Latin."

"I was a Greek merchant," interjected the ghost of Heraclitus, "and I think you should speak my Greek language, or at the very least know a few Greek curse words."

"I was a slave from Jerusalem," piped up another ghost. "I wanted to stay in Jerusalem, but a Roman soldier captured me, brought me to Carthage, and sold me here.

I'm your great-great-great-grandmother, Augustinus. How about you change your name to Jonah and learn some Hebrew like a good Jewish boy?"

More and more ghosts told their stories and tried to convince Augustinus to learn their language, until he

finally cried out: "You're all my ancestors, and I don't see why I should prefer one of you to the others. But I can't speak all your languages. That's impossible."

"So what's the solution?" asked the ghosts.

"I don't know!" said Augustinus. "You ghosts discuss it among yourselves. If you can reach an agreement about which language I should speak, let me know. Until then, I'm sticking with Latin."

The ghosts frowned. They didn't seem to like the idea, but they didn't have a better suggestion.

"In fact," added Augustinus, "there's a Latin sentence in a play by Terence, which you should all know. It says, *Homo sum: humani nihil a me alienum puto.* You know what it means?"

The ghosts who knew Latin smiled, but most of the others looked puzzled.

"It means," explained Augustinus, "**I am human, and nothing human is alien to me.** People in different countries often speak different languages. They also have different stories about gods, different art forms, and different food and games. But all people are human, and all humans can benefit from what any one human creates. True, Latin was first created by the Romans, theater by the Greeks, and stories about Jesus by the Jews. But Romans, Greeks, and Jews are all humans. And since I'm a human too, I can speak Latin, enjoy the theater, and learn from the wisdom of Jesus."

A NEW
EMPIRE

When an empire falls, the peoples it previously conquered don't simply gain their liberty back. Often these conquered peoples have changed so much that they no longer resemble their ancestors. Also, **when an empire falls, it's often simply replaced by another empire**. So when the Roman Empire fell, the Carthaginians didn't regain their independence. They were conquered by the Vandals. After some time, the Vandals were defeated by the Greeks, and Carthage became part of a new Greek

Empire, which—just to confuse everyone—called itself "the Roman Empire" because these Greeks said they were Romans. Finally, the Greek-Roman Empire was defeated by the Arabs who conquered Carthage and added it to the new Arab Empire.

At first the Carthaginians didn't like this Arab Empire. The Carthaginians spoke Latin and believed in the Christian religion, whereas the rulers of the Arab Empire spoke Arabic and believed in a new religion called Islam, preached by the prophet Muhammad. The Arabs also destroyed the city of Carthage and built a completely new city nearby—Tunis.

Over time, the descendants of Augustinus and the other Carthaginians got used to living in Tunis. They no longer thought of themselves as Carthaginians or Romans, they didn't speak Phoenician or Latin, and they didn't believe in Ba'al or Jesus. Instead, they spoke Arabic and believed in Muhammad and Islam. They came to think of themselves as Muslim Arabs and call themselves by Muslim names like Muhammad, Abdallah, and Fatima.

Hundreds of years later, a Muslim boy called Abdallah might have taken his herd of goats to pasture around the rubble of Carthage. As he walked over the ruins of Ba'al's temple and Christian churches, was he pestered by Augustinus's angry ghost? Would the ghost insist that the boy change his name, his language, and his religion? Or would the ghost just smile and whisper, *Homo sum: humani nihil a me alienum puto*?

HISTORY IS
COMPLICATED

We humans are lazy. When we have to think very hard about something, it gives us a headache. So we tend to like simple stories. We want stories in which it's easy to know who the good guys are and who the bad guys are. But history is complicated. **In the history of Carthage and Rome, for example, it's difficult to know for sure who was good and who was bad.** Was the famous general Hanniba'al good because he fought the Romans or bad because he destroyed so many cities in Spain and elsewhere?

Worse than that, it's difficult to even know who was Carthaginian and who was Roman. Carthaginians became Romans, while Romans became Carthaginians. Some people were both Carthaginian and Roman at the same time. And their great-great-grandchildren were no longer either Carthaginian or Roman—they became Tunisian.

That's one very important lesson from the history of empires. Simple stories are usually only in fairy tales. Real history is complicated. And **because we're all real people rather than fairy-tale characters, we're all complicated**. We think of our ancestors as one group of people, but like in Terence's plays, it turns out our ancestors aren't who we thought they were. We think we belong to just

one country, but actually we owe a lot to other countries. And if we go back in time, sooner or later we'll discover that some of our own ancestors were foreigners. More importantly, we like to think we're descended from the good guys of history. But to some extent, all of us are also descended from the bad guys. That's a very disturbing idea. Do you know of any bad guys in your country's history, or your family's?

Maybe the best conclusion is that we have to live with our ancestors' legacy, but even if we're descended from bad guys, we can behave differently from them. **If our ancestors fought wars and built empires, that doesn't mean we have to.** We can't change the past, and we shouldn't try to go back to how things were before the first empire was created—that's just impossible. But we don't have to repeat the past. No matter what our ancestors did, we are not our ancestors. We can be different.

4
THE MEANING
OF LIFE

THE ONE
TRUE STORY?

BOOKS, MOVIES, AND VIDEO GAMES ARE FULL OF STORIES ABOUT wars, battles, and empires because these are dramatic, attention-grabbing events. This leads some people to think wars are the only things that happen when foreigners meet. It's like when two kids get into a fight at school: All the other kids come to see what's going on, and that's all anyone can talk about for days afterward.

But the truth is that most of the time kids don't fight. Most of the time they get along quite well. It's the same with history. Most of the time when foreigners met, they didn't fight. They occasionally married, they often traded, and even more often they talked and told stories. They talked about what made them sad and what made them happy, and they shared stories about how the world was created, where humans and animals came from, and what rules everyone should follow. They told stories about the Roman gods Jupiter and Mars, the Carthaginian gods

Ba'al and Tanit, about the Sky Father and Jesus Christ, and about the Muslim prophet Muhammad.

Everybody believed their own story was true. But how could that be when there were so many different stories that sometimes contradicted each other? The Christians, for example, believed the Sky Father was the only real god and that he created the entire universe, but the Greeks believed in the gods Zeus and Artemis, and the Carthaginians believed in Ba'al and Tanit. They couldn't all be right.

You might experience something like this in your everyday life. Maybe you hear different stories about something that happened and don't know which to believe. Maybe two girls in school who were once best friends suddenly stopped talking to each other. One of them tells everyone it's because the other girl didn't invite her to her birthday party. The birthday girl says it's because the first girl was mean to her and spread nasty rumors about her. And a third girl—who was friends with both of them—says it actually all started because they fought over a boy. It isn't easy to know whom to believe.

It's the same with all the stories people told about gods, and the origin of humanity, and what happens after we die. Many people wanted to know which was the one true story. One person who really wanted to know this was Möngke Khan, the ruler of the Mongol Empire. He wasn't just a very curious person—he was also the most powerful man of his time.

AN INVITATION TO
KARAKORUM

Möngke Khan was the grandson of a great, violent conqueror called Genghis Khan. Hundreds of years after the Arabs established their empire and built Tunis, Genghis Khan, who may have killed more people than anyone before him, created an even bigger empire—the Mongol Empire. After Genghis died, Möngke Khan ruled the empire. He waged even more wars and made his empire even bigger. It stretched all the way from the Pacific Ocean to the Mediterranean, and from Korea to Ukraine.

But just like King Gilgamesh of Uruk, **Möngke Khan knew his power wouldn't last forever**. He knew he would die one day, and maggots would eat his body. Despite all his power, he didn't know how to defeat death. He didn't know where people came from or what life was all about. He heard many stories about it: He ruled a giant empire with lots of people, so he probably heard more stories than anyone in the world. And he wanted very much to know which of all these stories was true.

Maybe, Möngke Khan thought, he could arrange a big debate between the wisest people in the world, and these people could finally decide which stories were false and which was the one true story? And then **maybe he could make all the people in the world accept that one true story**, and then they would all obey him. One story, one khan.

So in the year 1254, Möngke Khan invited wise people from all over Asia, Europe, and Africa to a big conference in his capital city of Karakorum. If you're wondering why he didn't invite anyone from America or Australia... Well, at the time nobody knew the *whole* world. Möngke Khan had never heard of America and Australia, and people in America and Australia had never heard of Möngke Khan and his Mongol Empire.

Maybe one of the wise people who embarked on the long and perilous journey to Karakorum was Abdallah, the boy from Tunis, who'd grown up to be a famous Muslim scholar, an ulama. Imagine that he traveled with his daughter, Fatima, who was a bright and curious girl, and who loved nothing more than talking with her father and everybody else about the secrets of the world.

When they arrived at Karakorum, Abdallah went straight to Möngke Khan's palace to meet the other sages from Europe, Persia, India, and China. And while the grown-ups told their different stories to the khan, Fatima stayed at the inn. There she met kids from many different countries who had also come to the Karakorum conference with their fathers, mothers, or teachers.

"Hello," said Fatima to four kids she met at the inn. "I'm Fatima, and I'm from Tunis. I came here with my father, Abdallah."

"Hi," replied a boy. "My name's Paul, and I'm from Rome. I'm learning to become a Christian priest. My

teacher is at the palace telling Möngke Khan all about the Sky Father and Jesus Christ."

"Hey, I'm also learning to become a Christian priest," said another boy. "I'm Constantinus, and I'm from Ephesus."

"I'm Eleanor," said a shy girl who then immediately fell silent.

"And I'm Khulan," a second girl introduced herself. "I'm Mongolian. I was born here in Karakorum, and I'm very happy you all came here. Most people in my family believe in the ninety-nine Tengri gods and the spirits of earth and water, but I've heard a bit about other religions and I'd like to hear more. I've never left Karakorum, so I think I can learn a lot from meeting people from other countries."

"That's right," agreed Fatima. **"You always learn so many new and amazing things by talking to foreigners."**

"My teacher told me it's good to travel, even to the most distant lands," said Paul, "because so many people still haven't heard about the Sky Father. So that's what he does all his life—and it's what I want to do too. If everybody hears about the Sky Father and believes in him, then we could all agree on the same rules and everybody could live in peace."

"Interesting," said Khulan. "That's exactly what our khan wants too. One story for everybody, and one khan for everybody . . . So I'm all ears. What can you tell us about the Sky Father?"

"Well," said Paul in a very serious voice, "in the beginning the Sky Father created the whole universe and everything in it. He created the Earth and the sun and the moon, the oceans and the rainclouds and the volcanoes."

"And also the humans and the elephants and the spiders!" added Constantinus. "The Sky Father loves everything and everybody he created, so all the people in the world should follow his commands. It doesn't matter where you live or what language you speak. Like all other creatures, you too were created by the Sky Father, and he loves you—so you must obey his rules."

"And what rules did he give?" asked Khulan.

"You shouldn't kill anyone," said Paul, "and you shouldn't steal or lie."

"And you should help the poor and the sick," added Constantinus.

"Those sound like really good rules," Khulan said approvingly. "I already try to live by them. So I must be Christian too!"

"Not so fast," Paul and Constantinus said simultaneously. "There are other rules you must keep."

"Like, that skirt you're wearing is far too short," said Constantinus. "We can see your knees. The Sky Father doesn't like girls wearing short skirts."

Christians like Paul and Constantinus said that the Sky Father had given humans a very

126

long and detailed list of rules. There were rules about what you could wear, what you could eat, what games you could play, and which holidays you should celebrate. There were also rules about who should obey who.

"The young must obey the old," said Paul. "Women must obey men, and everybody must obey Christian priests."

"Christian priests," explained Constantinus, "are very close to the Sky Father and talk with him all the time. If you don't do what priests tell you, you'll make the Sky Father very angry, and he'll punish you. He might make a volcano erupt or send a terrible plague that makes people sick. So if Christian priests tell you to give money

toward building a big church for the Sky Father . . . you must give them money. And if they tell you to stop fighting another kingdom, you must make peace with it."

"And what happens," asked Khulan, "if I don't kill anyone and I help poor people, but I don't follow the other rules, like women having to wear long skirts and obey men?"

"If you did that," said Paul, "the Sky Father would be very angry with you and he would send you to a terrible place called hell. All the Sky Father's rules are equally important, and you can't only follow the rules you like."

Khulan fell silent and looked at Eleanor, who hadn't yet said a word.

WHAT IF I DON'T BELIEVE IN
THE SKY FATHER?

Over many centuries, Christian priests told stories like these to people in lots of different countries, and they still tell them today. Most countries in Europe—from Greece to Iceland, and from Ukraine to Ireland—became Christian. Many people in countries outside Europe also became Christian, like in Ethiopia in Africa and Lebanon in Asia. And in the modern age, when people from Europe began traveling to America and Australia, the Christian faith spread to more lands, like Mexico and Brazil and Fiji. **But people didn't always become Christians just because the Christian stories were convincing.** There was another reason.

"You Christians talk a lot about love and peace," Eleanor said, finally joining the discussion. "But Christians are sometimes very violent. For example, Constantinus, I've heard one of the most beautiful temples in the world—the temple of Artemis—once stood in your city of Ephesus, but the Christians destroyed it and used the stones to build a church."

"Of course," said Constantinus. "We want everyone to believe in the Sky Father alone, so we destroy temples to all the other gods and build churches instead."

"And that's a good thing!" interjected Paul. "We destroyed temples to other gods in Rome too, or turned them into churches. Because all these other gods, like Artemis, Ba'al, Zeus, and Jupiter don't really exist. They're just imaginary; they're stories invented by people."

"That's so mean!" said Khulan. "It's fine if you convince people to believe in the Sky Father. But *forcing* them to believe in your god and destroying all the other temples? That's . . . it's barbaric!"

"Pah," Paul snorted angrily. "Don't talk to me about barbarism! How many people has your khan massacred in all his wars, huh?"

"Fair point," said Khulan, slightly ashamed. "I don't think it's okay that our khan invades other countries and conquers their people. But at least we Mongols let everyone believe whatever they want. **After the Mongol army conquered the Christian lands around the city of Kyiv, we allowed the people there to go on being Christians.** I told you my family believes in the ninety-nine Tengri gods and the spirits of earth and water. What would your Christian king do to us if he ever conquers us?"

Paul smiled. "Well, wouldn't it be a good thing to get rid of all your superstitions? Ninety-nine gods and thousands of spirits? Who believes nonsense like that? It's just a bunch of primitive ghost stories your priests came

up with to trick you! Your gods and spirits don't really exist."

"Did it ever occur to you," Khulan asked pointedly, "that your Sky Father could be just a story your priests came up with?"

THE INQUISITION

When Christianity came to Rome, Carthage, Ephesus, and other places, many people became Christian, but plenty of others had their doubts, like Khulan. But the Christians became more numerous and powerful until it was dangerous to voice these doubts. Even though Christians kept saying that the Sky Father loved *everyone*, some Christians started hating the people who didn't believe in the Sky Father. And in countries that were ruled by Christians, **they sometimes switched from talking . . . to fighting**.

Instead of bringing peace to the world, the Sky Father story created a lot of new wars. Although Christians said, "The Sky Father told us not to kill anyone," they started killing people just for refusing to believe in the Sky Father. If someone said, "I don't believe your story," Christian priests might seize them, take them to the city's main square, and kill them in front of everyone. So people who

didn't believe in the Sky Father were soon afraid to even mention their doubts.

"There's something I'd like to tell you," Eleanor said to Paul and Constantinus, "but first you must promise not to beat me."

"Of course we won't beat you," they both replied. "Why would you think that?"

"Well," said Eleanor, "I've learned to be careful about what I say. I was born in the city of Béziers, in the south of France. One day, a large Christian army came to our city, captured it, and killed anyone who didn't believe in your Sky Father stories."

Paul and Constantinus fell silent and looked uneasily at the ground.

"But that's not all," continued Eleanor. "The Christian priests began to suspect that maybe they hadn't found everyone who didn't believe the Sky Father stories. Maybe people were so afraid of being killed that they *said* they believed the stories, even if they didn't."

"So what did the priests do?" asked Fatima and Khulan.

"They invented something they called the Inquisition," said Eleanor. "The Inquisition is the Christian priests' secret police. It's called the Inquisition because it constantly inquires if you really believe in the Sky Father stories. My parents were chatting in the kitchen one day, and my mother said she wasn't sure if the Sky Father stories were true, and my father admitted he wasn't convinced either. They thought it was a private conversation, just the two of them."

"And what happened?" asked Fatima and Khulan.

"A neighbor was passing by the kitchen window, and he heard what my parents were saying. He snitched on them to the Inquisition, and the Inquisition took them and . . . and . . . and burned them alive in the city's main square. I escaped with my older brother, and we fled as far as we could from the Christian priests, joining a caravan of merchants that brought us all the way here, to Karakorum."

Constantinus felt very bad. He turned to Eleanor and said, "I am so sorry about what happened to you. Yes, I've heard that some Christians do terrible things in distant places, like Rome and France, but I don't think that's really how the Sky Father wants people to behave. It's bad if people don't believe in the Sky Father, but it's even worse to kill people just because they don't believe in him. You know, not all Christians are the same. The Christians who did this to your family are called Catholics. I'm not Catholic. I'm Orthodox."

Paul, who was Catholic, looked angrily at Constantinus and said, "Wasn't it the Orthodox who destroyed Artemis's temple? I've heard the Orthodox destroyed plenty of other temples too *and* started entire wars with people who stayed loyal to their old gods. Don't pretend it's only Catholics who did things like that."

"I don't really get it," said Khulan, looking very sad. "Why do people fight and kill just because of gods?"

Before the Christians came up with their stories about the Sky Father, **people fought lots of wars, but they were rarely about gods**. Everybody had their own gods—like the ninety-nine Tengri gods, Ba'al and Tanit, Jupiter and Mars, or Zeus and Artemis—and everybody accepted that there were many different gods. If someone chose to worship different gods than yours, that was fine. Even when the Romans conquered the Greeks and Carthaginians, they didn't force everybody to abandon their gods and accept only the Roman gods. But once

Christians began saying there's only one god in the whole world, that's when they started fighting people who didn't believe in that one god.

WHAT THE SKY FATHER SAID
ABOUT KIDS

The Christians fought a lot of people who didn't believe in the Sky Father, but they also fought among themselves. Yes, all Christians believed in the Sky Father, but they started arguing about what exactly he told them to do. The more Paul and Constantinus talked together, the more they disagreed.

"When my father gets back from Möngke Khan's conference tonight," said Constantinus, "I'll ask him about what Eleanor told us."

"Your father?" Paul said with a slight sneer. "What's he doing here?"

"Isn't it obvious?" replied Constantinus. "He's one of the priests the khan invited. Everyone in Ephesus and the surrounding area says my father is the wisest priest in the world!"

"But how can a priest be your father?!" exclaimed Paul. "The Sky Father said priests mustn't marry or have kids! Your father broke the rules!"

"Liar!" shouted Constantinus. "The Sky Father never made a rule that priests shouldn't have kids!"

"Idiot!" screamed Paul. "Your father comes here to teach the Mongols about the Sky Father when he himself disobeys the Sky Father!"

"My father's the best priest in the world!" Constantinus yelled back. "Take back what you said or I'll punch you!"

One of the things Catholic and Orthodox Christians disagreed about the most was whether priests could marry and have children. The Orthodox thought this was fine, while Catholics thought the Sky Father strictly forbade this. Paul and Constantinus screamed louder and louder and even began hitting each other, until Fatima and Khulan intervened and stopped the fighting.

Much worse fights happened between Christians in many places. **Entire wars were fought over these disagreements.** All Christians agreed about some of the rules that the Sky Father had laid down, like not killing, but when they argued about the other rules . . . they sometimes ended up killing one another.

136

For example, fifty years before the Karakorum conference, there was a terrible battle in the big city of Constantinople. A Catholic army that believed the Sky Father forbade priests to have kids attacked the city, which was ruled by Orthodox Christians who believed the Sky Father allowed priests to have kids. Of course, they didn't fight only about whether priests could have kids: Constantinople was an extremely rich city, and many of the attackers just wanted to steal its wealth. They all agreed that the Sky Father said it's bad to steal, but they did it anyway. The Catholic Christians captured the city, burned entire neighborhoods, looted the Orthodox Christian churches of their gold and silver, and killed thousands of Orthodox Christians.

WHAT THE SKY FATHER SAID
ABOUT WINE

There were also people who believed in the Sky Father but weren't Christian at all. They usually called the Sky Father by the name Allah, and agreed that he created the whole universe but claimed that almost everything else the Catholic and Orthodox Christians said about the Sky Father was wrong. These people were Muslims, like Fatima and her father Abdallah.

"I'm glad you stopped fighting at last," said Fatima.

"I've been listening carefully, and I agree with some of the things you said. I believe in the Sky Father too. But my father says that your Christian priests tell lots of lies about the Sky Father."

Paul and Constantinus stopped glowering at each other and turned to Fatima.

"What lies?" they asked.

"For example," said Fatima, "Christian priests tell people that the Sky Father likes wine, and you should do a special ritual in honor of the Sky Father when you drink wine."

"That's right!" said Paul and Constantinus, who were glad there was something they could agree on. Constantinus explained, "That wine is like the blood of Jesus Christ, the Sky Father's son. By drinking the blood of Christ, you connect with the Sky Father."

"But actually," said Fatima, "the Sky Father made a very important rule that nobody should ever drink wine. If you drink wine, you'll make the Sky Father very angry, and he'll send you to hell."

Paul and Constantinus looked at Fatima and shook their heads.

"Christian priests also claim the Sky Father said it's okay to eat pork."

"Yup," said Paul and Constantinus. "We like pork."

"But actually," said Fatima, "the Sky Father made a rule that nobody should ever eat pork. If you eat pork, you'll make the Sky Father very angry."

"We don't think so," disagreed Paul and Constantinus.

"The Sky Father made another important rule," continued Fatima. "For one month a year—a month called Ramadan—you shouldn't eat or drink anything at all during the day. You can only eat and drink at night. But Christian priests never talk about this rule, which makes the Sky Father very angry."

"You must have made that one up," said Paul.

"Yes, I've never heard about that rule!" exclaimed Constantinus.

"That's because you listen to Christian priests," said Fatima. "You should listen only to the Muslim ulama instead. They know what the Sky Father really wants."

As you can imagine, Christians didn't like being told this. **Even though Christians and Muslims both believed that the Sky Father created everything, they couldn't agree on much else.**

The first Muslims were mostly Arab people who lived in the Arabian desert, near Phoenicia. Like Christians, Muslims went to many other countries to spread their stories about the Sky Father, and today there are many countries in which most people are Muslim, such as Senegal and Mali in West Africa, Egypt and Iran in the

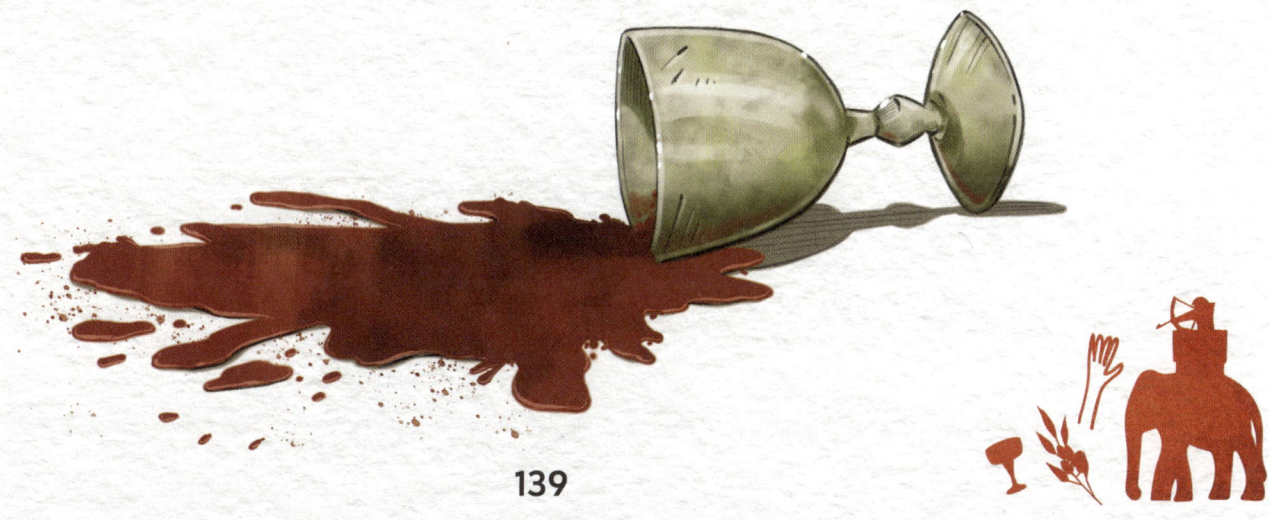

Middle East, and Bangladesh and Indonesia in South Asia. Some people in these countries became Muslims because they were convinced by the Muslim stories. But just like the Christians, Muslims didn't like it when anyone refused to believe their stories, and they sometimes switched from talking to fighting.

"Tell me, Fatima," Eleanor interjected quietly. "What happens if someone in a Muslim country doesn't believe in the Sky Father at all?"

Fatima hesitated, then she admitted she'd heard that such people were persecuted and sometimes killed just because they didn't believe in the Sky Father.

"I see," said Eleanor, looking quite sad.

Both Christian and Muslim stories about the Sky Father spread around the world and brought about a lot of changes, like introducing new holidays for people to celebrate. For example, Christians all over the world began observing Christmas, a holiday that celebrated the birth of Jesus Christ. People also began speaking in new languages. Muslims in places like Egypt and Tunisia, for example, started speaking Arabic—the language of the first Muslims and of the prophet Muhammad.

People even changed what they wore and ate and drank. For example, Muslims stopped eating pork and drinking wine. But if people hoped that the Sky Father stories would bring peace to the world, they were very disappointed. The stories actually seemed to cause even more wars than before.

THE BIG PROBLEM WITH
THE SKY FATHER

"You know," Khulan said to Fatima, Paul, and Constantinus, "you three at least agree on one thing—the Sky Father created the whole universe and everything in it, and he knows everything and can do anything he wants."

"Right," agreed Fatima, Paul, and Constantinus.

"But if that's true, why is there so much suffering in the world? If the Sky Father can do anything he wants, why doesn't he stop all the wars? Why does he let people hurt and even kill each other?"

"I don't think it's the Sky Father's fault that there are wars," said Paul. "It's the bad people who start these wars. It's their fault."

"But even if some bad people decide to start a war," said Khulan, "surely the Sky Father could still stop the war and protect good people from the bad people, right?"

"I've heard that this is all just a test," said Constantinus. "The Sky Father created a wonderful place called heaven, where nothing bad ever happens, there are no wars and no pain and no death, and people live forever in perfect joy and happiness. But to decide who gets into heaven, the Sky Father also created the Earth. Here on Earth, we live for just a very short time, and the Sky Father watches us closely—he watches everything we do. If we do good things, then the Sky Father takes us to heaven when we

die. If we do bad things, the Sky Father doesn't let us into heaven. So even if good people sometimes suffer on Earth, it doesn't matter because it's just for a few years, and then they get to live in heaven forever!"

"That's not very convincing," replied Khulan. "How can we possibly know if it's true? Do you know anyone who came back from heaven to prove that it really exists?"

"Umm . . ." said Constantinus. "Not really."

"Besides," continued Khulan, "if the Sky Father created everything and can do anything, why does he bother with this complicated test? He could have just created good people and put them all in heaven right away and not bothered creating any bad people in the first place."

"Hmm," said Fatima hesitantly, "that's a good point, Khulan. When my poor mother suddenly fell ill and died last year, I had similar thoughts. Even if wars are caused by bad people rather than the Sky Father, what about

things like disease or earthquakes? They aren't caused by bad people, right? If the Sky Father created everything and can do anything, why did he create the disease that killed my mother?"

"I'm so sorry to hear about your mother," said Khulan, putting a hand on Fatima's shoulder. "And you know, it isn't just humans who suffer from diseases, earthquakes, and violence. Millions of animals suffer too. Gazelles get eaten by tigers. Chicks get torn to pieces by eagles. Baby elephants get lost in the desert and die of thirst. Puppies get lost on the streets of a city and die of hunger. If the Sky Father is perfectly good and can do anything he wants, **why did he create a world with so much suffering in it?** Do you think the poor gazelles and lost puppies also go to heaven?"

TWO
GODS

Wherever people who believed in the Sky Father met, they often discussed these difficult questions. They thought about them very hard, but their answers weren't very convincing. However, there were other people, people who didn't believe in the Sky Father, who actually had **a simple answer to all these questions**.

"I know why there's so much suffering in the world," said Eleanor.

"Why?" asked all the others.

"Both Christians and Muslims are wrong when they say there's just one big god who created the entire world. Actually, there are two big gods! There's the good Prince of Light, and the evil Prince of Darkness—the Devil. The Prince of Light created everything good—joy and love, and nice animals like lambs and butterflies. The Devil created everything bad—pain and hate, and vicious animals like tigers and eagles. It's the Devil who's responsible for wars and diseases."

The others were listening attentively. "That's very interesting," said Paul.

"Yes, please go on," said Fatima.

"The Prince of Light is constantly fighting the Devil, trying to stop him. When Light wins, good things happen. When the Devil wins, bad things happen—like what happened to my family, and to your mother, Fatima. The Prince of Light is very powerful, but he still can't do absolutely anything he wants because the Devil's also very powerful. We humans should help the Prince of Light defeat the Devil, and then there'll be no more pain or war or disease."

"And how can we help the Prince of Light?" asked Fatima.

"By doing good things," answered Eleanor, "like being nice to people instead of hurting them."

The story of the Prince of Light and the Devil was very ancient; people first told it in the land of Persia more than 1,000 years before the Karakorum conference. Back then, they called the good god Ahura Mazda, and they called the evil god Angra Mainyu. Over the years the names of the two gods changed. Sometimes people called the evil god Ahriman, Satan, Lucifer, Iblis, or the Devil. But the story remained roughly the same. It was a very convincing story, and it had one really big advantage over the Sky Father story. This story about two gods easily explained why so many bad things happened in the world—including to good people.

It was such a convincing story that even Christians and Muslims began repeating it. They still said there's just one big god, the Sky Father, who created everything and can do anything he wants, but whenever people asked, "So why are there wars and diseases?" they would say, "Oh, that's because of the Devil."

In truth, it didn't make much sense for Christians and Muslims who believed in the Sky Father to believe in the Devil as well. If, as Christians and Muslims claimed, the Sky Father created everything and could do

anything he wanted, then why did he create the Devil? And **why didn't he just get rid of the Devil?** Christians and Muslims had no convincing answer to that question. But people have a way of believing things that don't make much sense . . . so lots of Christians and Muslims somehow managed to believe in both the Sky Father who can do anything he wants and the Devil who causes all the problems in the world.

A THIRD GOD?

"So let me get this straight," Paul said to Eleanor. "You don't believe there's a single great god who controls the whole world?"

"No," agreed Eleanor.

"Instead, you believe there are two gods—one good, one bad—who fight to control the world?"

"Yes," agreed Eleanor.

"But that doesn't make any sense!" said Paul.

"Why not?" asked Eleanor.

"Well," said Paul, "if the world is a battlefield for two opposing gods, then who decides the rules of the battle? Who decides what the good god and evil god need to do in order to win?"

"What do you mean?" Eleanor was puzzled.

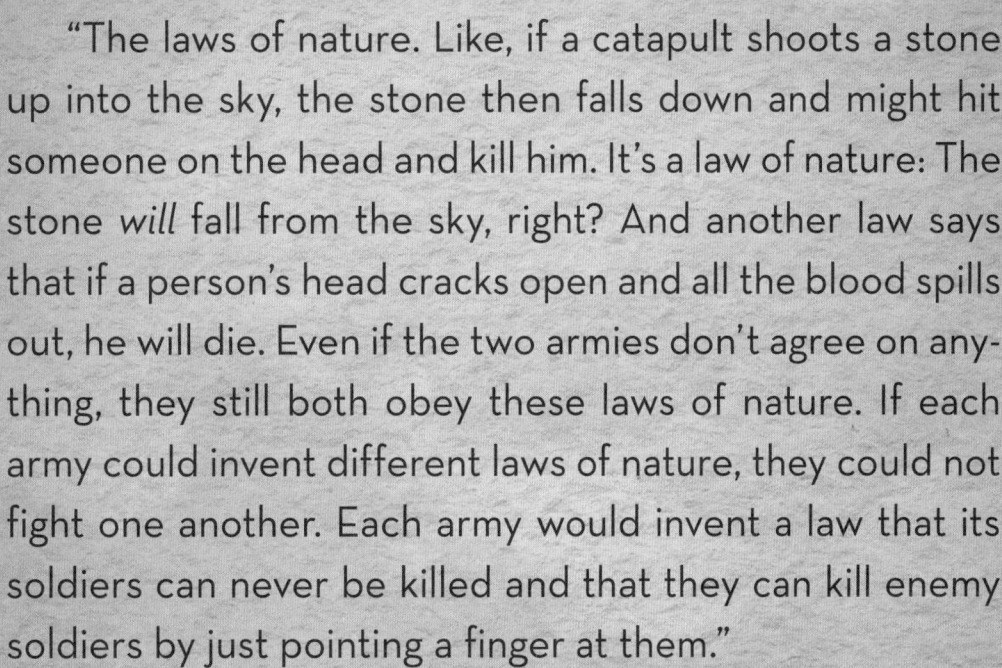

"Suppose two armies go to war," explained Paul. "They can fight each other only because they both obey some laws, which they can't change."

"What laws?" Eleanor asked.

"The laws of nature. Like, if a catapult shoots a stone up into the sky, the stone then falls down and might hit someone on the head and kill him. It's a law of nature: The stone *will* fall from the sky, right? And another law says that if a person's head cracks open and all the blood spills out, he will die. Even if the two armies don't agree on anything, they still both obey these laws of nature. If each army could invent different laws of nature, they could not fight one another. Each army would invent a law that its soldiers can never be killed and that they can kill enemy soldiers by just pointing a finger at them."

"But in our world," continued Paul, "there *are* wars and soldiers *do* fight and sometimes kill each other because they can't change the laws of nature. The laws of nature are there, and everybody must obey them whether they like it or not. But if the whole universe was created by two gods who are constantly fighting, which one created the laws of nature, and which one decided the laws they must obey in their fight? If the Prince of Light made the laws, he would obviously make laws that work in his favor. If the Devil made the rules, he would make evil rules that helped him win every time."

"I see your point," said Eleanor. "So it looks like someone else made the laws. Someone more powerful than the Prince of Light and the Devil, who can make them both obey his rules."

"But wait," interjected Khulan, "that means the universe wasn't created by the Prince of Light and the Devil, and neither of them made the laws that govern everything. There's someone more powerful than them who created the universe."

"But who is that very powerful someone who both the Prince of Light and the Devil obey?" Fatima wondered out loud. "Is she a third god who created the Prince of Light and the Devil? And if so, why did this third god create a world with so much suffering in it?"

"Maybe the third god who created the world just doesn't care about us and our suffering," said Eleanor. "Maybe she enjoys tormenting the people and animals she created, like a kid who pulls the wings off flies and laughs at their suffering. Maybe there's just one god who created everything—and she's evil."

The kids fell silent, no longer sure what to think. They couldn't tell which of all the different stories about various gods was true. And the exact same thing happened to the adults who were debating the same questions in the khan's palace: The wise people argued for a very long time and couldn't agree whether there were many gods, two gods, or just one god, and who that one god was. The khan never got his answer.

WHY DO WE **SUFFER?**

All the different stories people told about gods didn't seem to explain the world, bring peace to the world, or protect people from suffering. So some wise persons said there was no point arguing about gods. Why did it matter if there were lots of gods or one or two or none at all? Instead of arguing about gods, people should try to find out what was causing all the suffering in the world—and how it could be stopped.

One person who thought like this was a young man called Siddhartha, who lived in India more than 1,500 years before Möngke Khan organized his conference in Karakorum. Siddhartha was a prince, and he grew up in a palace. From an early age, **he wanted to understand why there was so much misery in the world**. A bit like Möngke Khan, Siddhartha talked with many people from different lands.

He always asked people what the deepest cause of their misery was. Many of them said they were miserable because they didn't have enough money or enough land or enough food. "If I were rich and famous," they said, "I'd be perfectly happy! That's why I pray to my gods every day to make me rich and famous!"

Many, many people said the same thing, but it didn't sound right. As a prince who lived in a palace, Siddhartha knew the richest, most famous, and most powerful people of his time. He often met wealthy people, high priests, and even kings. And he noticed that they weren't always happy, despite having a lot of money, land, and food.

Some rich people had heaps of gold and silver, large houses, all the delicacies they could eat, and many servants and slaves who did everything they commanded. Yet they weren't happy. They were jealous of people who were even wealthier than them. They were afraid robbers might steal their gold or a disease would ruin their crops. They were even more afraid that the king would take away all their land and money.

Siddhartha knew a few kings too. Some kings ruled big empires and had tens of thousands of soldiers at their command, and still they weren't happy. They were jealous of kings with bigger empires or more soldiers. They were afraid some other king would take their empire, and they were even more afraid one of their own soldiers would murder them and make himself king.

Then there were the priests. Siddhartha met priests who claimed to know everything about the world. They said they knew which gods ruled the world, what these gods wanted, and how to pray to them to get their help. "If you pray to the right god," said these priests, "eat the food he orders you to eat and fast on days he orders you to fast, then he will help you and you'll be a very happy person."

Yet even these priests weren't always happy. They were enraged when other priests contradicted them and told different stories. They were afraid the king might listen to some other priest, and they were even more afraid they were perhaps wrong about what they believed and didn't really know everything about the world.

Siddhartha noticed that **jealousy, anger, and fear—the things that made life miserable even for the rich, for kings, and for priests—were the same everywhere**. The wealthy in every country were jealous. Kings in every country were afraid. Priests in every country got angry. It didn't matter where they lived, what language they spoke, or which gods they believed in.

Siddhartha also noticed something very strange: It is not foreigners from a distant land who often make us miserable but rather the people we love most in the world. Our parents hurt us, like when they shout and punish us. Our brothers and sisters hurt us, like when they tease us or take our toys. Our friends hurt us, like when they laugh at us or refuse to play with us. And we often hurt them back. "That's very strange," thought Siddhartha. "Why would people who love each other hurt each other?"

Nobody seemed to know the answer to his questions or how to end all this suffering. So Siddhartha decided to explore these things himself, and **what he discovered changed the world**. People started calling him Buddha, which means "the one who knows the way out of

suffering," and even today there are millions of people who believe in what he discovered. In Karakorum in 1254, there were also people who knew Buddha's story.

MY WORST ENEMY

After talking with the other kids at the inn, Fatima was quite troubled. She went for a walk outside by herself and was thinking about why there was so much suffering in the world, when somebody called out to her:

"Hey, you! Stop!"

Fatima stopped and saw a boy in a saffron robe.

"Why did you shout at me?" she asked.

"You almost stepped on an ant," said the boy. "Sorry I startled you. I'm Anand."

"Oh," said Fatima, a little baffled. "I was so deep in thought I didn't notice you or the ant. I'm Fatima, by the way. And, uh, why do you care so much about that ant?"

"Ants feel pain too, you know. That's what I learned from my teacher."

"Who's your teacher? One of the Christian priests or the Muslim ulama? If you care about the pain of something as small as an ant, maybe you and your teacher can tell me why there's so much suffering in the world."

"My teacher's a famous sage from the island of Sri

Lanka," said Anand. "He teaches people what Buddha discovered. We're in Karakorum because of this conference the khan organized, not that I'm very interested in the arguments at the khan's palace. I'm just trying to understand what causes all the suffering in the world. But I don't think I'm getting very far. It's just so complicated! I mean, of course I understand some things about suffering. Like, everyone knows we sometimes suffer because of things others do to us."

"Right," agreed Fatima. "That's easy. Sometimes enemies from another country invade, and that makes us miserable. Or a bully humiliates us, and we feel miserable. And when my father shouts at me, then I feel really miserable!"

"But have you noticed, Fatima, **that we're sometimes miserable because of things we do to ourselves**? My teacher says the person who hurts me most in the world isn't a foreigner, a neighbor, or even a brother or a parent—it's me."

"Really? Why would I hurt myself?" Fatima asked.

"Well, suppose you have some work to do before you can go outside and play with your friends. The best thing would be to finish the work quickly so you can go play, right?"

"Right!" said Fatima, "Like when my father gives me math problems to solve and says I can't go out till I solve them. He really wants me to be good at math."

"And do you ever find that when you're trying to focus

on your math problem, you start thinking instead about your friends already having fun outside while you're stuck inside with math? That probably makes it even harder for you to focus, so it takes you longer to solve the math problem, which means you can't join your friends. And maybe you get angry at your dad for giving you the math problem...."

"That's so true!" exclaimed Fatima. "And I'm angry at myself too. I don't understand why I keep thinking about my friends outside instead of focusing on the math problem. If I could just concentrate on the problem, I know I could solve it just like that and then go out to play! I sometimes yell at the thoughts in my head, telling them to leave me alone, but they just stay there annoying me."

"That happens to me too," Anand admitted. "And no matter how hard I try, I don't understand where the annoying thoughts come from. Who makes them?"

$$\{[(6 \cdot 4) + 7^2] \cdot \sqrt{9} - (\tfrac{1}{3} \cdot 18) - 60 + 40 - (7 \cdot \pi \cdot \sqrt{a} \cdot 0) + \sqrt{100} - (3 \cdot 10 \cdot \tfrac{2}{3}) - 5 + 0 - 32\} \cdot b \cdot c = \;?$$

"That's a good question," said Fatima. "In my case, it's definitely not my dad who makes the annoying thoughts in my head. Do I come up with them myself? But they make me miserable. **Why would I create thoughts that make me miserable?**"

"That's what my teacher keeps asking me," said Anand. "But I can't find the answer. Like, a year ago, my best friend Tashi insulted me in front of all the other kids. We were all eating this cake, and Tashi said I eat like a pig, and everyone laughed at me. Tashi only said it that one time a year ago, and he's probably forgotten about it. But for some reason, I keep remembering it. Sometimes the memory pops up out of nowhere: 'Hey, he said I eat like a pig! And everybody laughed at me!' And every time I remember it, I feel humiliated all over again."

"And you can't stop thinking about it?" asked Fatima.

"I can't! It's really weird. I get why our enemies want to harm us, but why would our own thoughts and memories want to? And why can't we stop them? I mean, I control my legs and eyes—**so why can't I control my thoughts and memories?** When I go to bed, I can tell my legs to relax and my eyes to shut, so why can't I tell my thoughts to stop? My teacher says it's because my mind's weak, and I should do more exercises."

"You mean like skipping with a rope and doing head-stands and stuff?"

"No, I mean exercises for the mind," Anand explained. "For example, my teacher tells me to close my eyes and

focus on breathing. I have to feel the breath coming into my nose and then feel it going out of my nose. I need to do this for an hour a day. And if any angry memories or annoying thoughts pop up into my mind, I should ignore them and keep focusing on the breath."

"And does it work?" Fatima asked.

"Just a little," admitted Anand. "Usually, after about a minute, or even just a few seconds, I start thinking about what I'll have for dinner or I remember how Tashi and the others laughed at me, and I forget all about my breathing. But my teacher says I should keep doing the exercise because it teaches me a very important lesson about why we suffer so much in life."

"And what's that?" Fatima said, eager to hear the answer.

"It teaches us that we don't really understand what's going on inside us. We don't know where thoughts, memories, and feelings come from, and since we have no

control over them, we often hurt the people we love, and we even hurt ourselves. Tashi didn't want to hurt me when he said I eat like a pig—he was probably just greedy and wanted a bigger piece of cake for himself, so he blurted the first thing that came into his head. And I definitely don't want to keep remembering what he said, but I can't control my memories, and they make me feel angry. And sometimes when I'm angry, it's like a kettle boiling over and spilling hot water everywhere—my anger makes me mean, even to my friends, and I end up making *them* miserable. Thoughts and memories keep popping into our minds and filling us with greed or anger, and when we're full of greed or anger there's no way we can be happy. Even the worst wars in the world start not with any evil gods but with angry memories and greedy thoughts in people's heads."

This was what Buddha discovered thousands of years ago, and it has been true of all the people who ever lived in the world. **No matter what gods people worship and what language they speak, they often feel greed and anger in their mind, and this makes them miserable.** It also makes them hurt the people around them instead of cooperating to overcome natural disasters like plagues and earthquakes. This is true of Indians and Chinese, of Romans and Persians, of Christians and Muslims. They all feel greed and anger, and then they hurt themselves and hurt others. It's even true of animals like tigers and eagles.

A WAY OUT

Buddha wanted to know why all this was happening. What decides which thought or memory comes up when? He looked very closely at what was going on inside him, and where all the greed and anger came from. He discovered that there wasn't some god producing these feelings. Every person and every animal is constantly producing greed and anger in our own minds. And then the greed and anger make us miserable, and make us spread misery around us by hurting others. And when the others get miserable, they hurt us back and make us even more miserable. That's how misery grows and multiplies.

"So is *that* what causes all the suffering in the world?" Fatima said. "Is this why there are so many wars and why people can still be miserable, even in peacetime?"

"That's what my teacher says," said Anand. "It isn't because of some evil god. We're doing it to ourselves. As long as we keep producing greed and anger and all kinds of annoying thoughts, we can't be happy—not even if we're a big emperor like Möngke Khan with millions of gold coins and thousands of soldiers. The khan's army can defeat and kill every enemy the khan has, except one—the annoying thoughts in the khan's own head."

"Can we stop producing greed and anger?" Fatima mused. "Can I perhaps produce joy instead of greed and

love instead of anger? If I could learn how to produce joy and love instead of greed and anger, I think I could be happy even if I didn't have a single gold coin or a single soldier."

"My teacher said that's exactly what Buddha did. For many years he practiced how to produce joy and love instead of greed and anger. And he discovered that it's just like training your body to swim or your mouth and fingers to play the flute and produce beautiful music—you can also train your mind to produce love rather than hate."

Buddha trained many people to produce love rather than hate, and they went from country to country and trained more people all over the world. They went from India to China, Japan, Thailand, and Vietnam, even to Europe and America. Today there are men and women in almost every country who try to practice what Buddha taught, and they're mostly called Buddhists.

But it's a very difficult practice. To become a champion swimmer or an expert flute player, you must practice every day for many years. Similarly, **you need to train very hard if you want to produce love instead of hate**. Practicing what Buddha taught was so difficult that even people who thought he discovered something good didn't do what he taught. Many Buddhists kept producing lots of greed and anger in their minds, and kept hurting others, fighting wars, and killing people. Some Buddhists even got so angry if someone refused to believe that Buddha had found a way to overcome anger that they would beat that person up or kill them.

LIBERTY

When Buddha taught people about his findings, he didn't forbid them to believe in gods. He just said that it was pointless to argue about gods and more important to find a way out of suffering. Buddha wasn't the only person in history to think like this. In recent years, many people have reached similar conclusions. They think there's no way all the people in the world can agree about what god to worship, what food to eat, what clothes to wear, and so forth. So instead of wasting a lot of time and energy arguing and fighting about these things, everyone in the world should agree on just one basic rule: Do your best to help others instead of harming them. If you keep to this single rule, you should be at liberty to do anything else you want, eat anything you fancy, dress however you please, and believe in as many or as few gods as you like.

This single rule allows people so much liberty that the people who follow it are often called "liberals." The word "liberal" comes from the Latin word "libertas," which means "liberty" or "freedom." According to liberals*, being a good person has nothing to do with obeying gods. Being

---

* In the present-day United States, many people associate the term "liberal" with supporters of the Democratic Party. But for centuries, the term had a much broader meaning, and supporters of many different political parties were proud to say they hold liberal views.

good means not harming anyone. You can of course still believe in gods—and there are many liberals who are also Christian or Muslim. But you can be a good person even if you don't believe in any god. Liberals argue that when we're trying to decide whether it's good to do something, it's pointless arguing about gods. Instead, we should ask whether what we want to do will hurt anyone. **As long as we don't hurt anyone, we should have the liberty to do what we want.**

For example, liberals agree with Christians and Muslims that you shouldn't kill anyone. But not because some god forbade it or because you're afraid of going to hell. No, liberals explain that "you shouldn't kill because this would cause terrible suffering to anyone you kill, and to their family and friends. In fact, it would even cause you a lot of suffering. So even if there are no gods in the world, you shouldn't kill."

Now what about clothes? Some people say that everybody must wear a certain type of hat on their head because a great god said so. But what if you want to wear a different kind of hat or no hat at all? This doesn't hurt

anyone, right? So liberals say: "You are at liberty to wear whatever hat you want."

Some people say there's a certain day of the year when nobody's allowed to eat because God wants us to fast on that day. But what if you're very hungry and you want to eat on that day? It wouldn't hurt anyone. So liberals say: "If you want to fast, you're at liberty to do that, but if you want to eat, you're free to do that too. As long as you don't hurt anyone, you can do anything you want."

The liberal rule sounds like a very good rule, but unfortunately liberals themselves have not always kept it. In some cases liberals even started entire wars to force other people to follow the liberal rule and avoid hurting others. Talking is much easier than doing. It's easy to *say* you believe in a rule—whether a Christian, Muslim, or liberal rule—but it's much harder to actually follow it. And it's not what people say that matters—it's what they do.

TALKING IS EASY; DOING IS HARD

There's a story about two neighbors—Baba and Gugu—who fell sick with a disease and each went to a different doctor. Baba's doctor said, "Eat an orange in the morning,

another orange in the afternoon, and a third orange in the evening—and you'll be cured within a month." To be sure Baba didn't forget the instructions, the doctor wrote them on a piece of paper and gave it to Baba.

Gugu's doctor gave Gugu a bottle full of pills and said, "Take one pill in the morning, one pill in the afternoon, and one pill in the evening—and you'll be cured within a month." To be sure Gugu didn't forget the instructions, the doctor wrote them on a piece of paper and gave it to Gugu.

When Baba and Gugu met on the way home, they told each other what their doctors had said. Then they started arguing.

"Oranges!" cried Gugu. "That's utter nonsense. You can't cure this disease with oranges. Look what it says on the paper my doctor gave me—pills!"

"But on the paper *my doctor* wrote, it clearly says oranges!" insisted Baba.

"Your doctor's stupid!"

"How dare you insult my doctor!" Baba replied angrily. "He's the best doctor in the world! Your doctor's the stupid one. Those pills he gave you will probably make you even more sick!"

"My pills are amazing!" shouted Gugu.

"My oranges are a million times better than your pills!" screamed Baba. "Your doctor's a complete idiot, and so are you for believing him!"

Gugu got so angry he slapped Baba across the face. Baba slapped him back, and soon they were rolling on the floor, kicking, punching, and pulling each other's hair. They fought on and on, and Gugu never took his pills, and Baba didn't eat a single orange.

That's often what happens in the world. **People have very strong opinions about how everybody should behave, and they argue and fight about it—without bothering to follow their own rules.** Some people talk a lot about love . . . but are actually full of hate. Some people say they believe in peace . . . but then they start wars.

Some people say the most important rule is not to hurt others . . . and then make everyone around them miserable. Maybe you know someone who tries to convince other people to follow some rule but they themselves break that rule.

HOW THEY
BECAME US

Over thousands of years, different people came up with lots of different rules and lots of different stories to justify their rules. It's hard to say which were the best rules and which were the truest stories. People are still arguing

about it today, just as they argued in Möngke Khan's palace in Karakorum. And sometimes they still fight about it like Constantinus and Paul in the inn at Karakorum. Even worse, some people still harm or even kill anyone who refuses to believe their stories.

People also keep changing their minds about all these things. They keep changing their beliefs, their languages, their clothes, and their food. The world isn't divided into neat boxes that always stay the same, as the box-people claim. The boxes keep mixing and changing all the time. Sometimes this involves a lot of violence, like when one country conquers another, burning cities and enslaving people. Sometimes it happens peacefully, like when someone comes to trade in the market or falls in love with a foreigner. But whichever way it happens and no matter where you live, **you owe much to many different people who lived in lots of foreign countries**!

If people in your family believe in a god, this is probably because foreigners from a different country once introduced your ancestors to that god. The same is true of the language you speak. Almost all the languages that people speak today came to our ancestors from a different country. Most of the words we use first came from some foreigner.

For example, more than half of all English words were borrowed from other languages like French, Latin, and Greek. The English word "music" came from the French

word "musique," which came from the Latin word "musica," which came from the Greek word "mousike." Even the English word "language" actually came from the French word "langue" which came from the Latin word "lingua." Try picturing a long line of people handing a word from one to the other until it finally reaches your ear—and then comes out of your mouth.

It's the same with the food you put *into* your mouth. A lot of it might be grown by foreigners. But even the food that people grow and make in your country was probably first discovered by a foreigner in a faraway land. For example, do you like chocolate? The first people who learned to turn cocoa beans into tasty treats lived more than 5,000 years ago in the tropical forests of Amazonia. Every time you put a piece of chocolate in your mouth, you should thank these ancient Amazonians.

Do you like tea? Thousands of years ago, people in China discovered how to make tea by pouring hot water on the leaves of tea trees. They called the drink "té" or "chá." From China, the love of tea spread far and wide. Today people grow tea trees in many other countries like India, Kenya, and Argentina, and tea is now the most common drink in the world—besides water! Everyone who drinks tea today should be grateful to the ancient Chinese for it.

Do you like your chocolate and your tea sweet? Then you should thank the people of New Guinea because 8,000 years ago they were the first to grow sugarcane and make sugar from it.

Now think about the games you like to play. Soccer was invented by the British, tae kwon do by Koreans, and chess by Indians. So when you kick a ball into the goal, you're being a little British; when you practice tae kwon do, that's your Korean side; and when you move your chess pawns, that's your connection to India.

It's the same with the music you listen to, the television series you watch, and the books you read. They all come from different countries. The book you are reading right now was also written and illustrated by foreigners from Israel, Germany, and Spain.

So being different or foreign can't be that bad. If all the people in your country were exactly the same, and if you could use only the things made by people from your

own country, what would your life be like? You and your family would sit at a table with not much food, and you wouldn't have many games to play with them or words to say to them.

In fact, even your family's full of people who came from different countries. If you went back in time to meet your grandmother, and her grandmother, and *her* grandmother, sooner or later you'd meet a foreigner: somebody who lived in a distant land, who believed in gods you don't know, and who spoke a language you don't understand. It's not just gods, food, games, and words that came to your country from elsewhere. People themselves made the journey. Some people arrived ten years ago, some a hundred years ago, and others came thousands of years ago. **Nobody was born out of the earth—or from dragon's teeth.**

Everybody's family came from somewhere else at some point in history. Our ancestors were once very different from us. Over time, these different people changed and became us. And we'll keep changing, so our descendants will also be very different from us.

The box-people are afraid of change because they think different people can't get along and always fight, but that's not true. Sure, people sometimes fight . . . but not necessarily because they're different. People often fight with the people most like themselves—their own family members, for example. On the other hand,

foreigners who are extremely different from one another sometimes get along just fine and even fall in love and start a new family. Even enemies can become friends.

THE BIGGEST DISCOVERY IN HISTORY

So now you know that being different isn't bad: Different people can get along well, and anyway, everything and everyone becomes different over time. You know that when foreigners meet, they sometimes trade, they sometimes fight, and they sometimes talk—but they always change. You know that no matter who we are, our ancestors were once foreigners, and they gradually turned into who we are now. You know that our ancestors may have done some very bad things, but we can behave differently from them.

You also know how to make rotten fish sauce, you know what an empire is, you know

how money works, and you know why it would be a terrible thing if everything you touched turned to gold. You know that the Romans first conquered the Greeks and Jews, but then helped spread Greek theater and the Jewish belief in the Sky Father.

You know lots of stories about gods, dragons, and ants. You know that the story of the Sky Father doesn't explain why good people suffer. You know that the story of the Prince of Light and the Devil doesn't explain how these two gods can fight each other. And you know that despite all the stories people told, they still found it very difficult to understand what was happening in the world—and even more difficult to understand what was happening inside their own bodies and heads. How do diseases start? Why do thoughts pop into our heads? Where do greed and anger come from?

People couldn't agree where humans themselves came from or how the world was created in the first place. They couldn't agree on why there was so much suffering in the world and what could be done about it. **Different people told different stories, and everyone was sure their own story was true.** But the only thing that was true of all people everywhere is that no matter what story they believed, they still suffered from famine, disease, and war. People everywhere talked a lot about these problems . . . but nobody actually managed to solve them.

Then some people made the biggest discovery in all of history, and it changed just about everything. It helped people explore the whole world, and even what was happening inside their bodies and heads. It also helped people decide which stories to believe.

This big discovery was science. Science is the method we use today to work out which stories to believe, to explore what causes war, and to find solutions for famine and disease. Science helps us research how thoughts and feelings emerge, and where we humans came from in the first place.

It's thanks to science that this book itself was written and that we today know so much about people in ancient Carthage, the Roman Empire, and the days of Jesus, Buddha, and Möngke Khan. The archaeologists who dig up ancient ships and study their cargo and who discovered the lost cities of Uruk, Carthage, Ephesus, and Karakorum are scientists. Other scientists devote their lives to learning ancient languages like Latin and to studying ancient stories about forgotten gods like Inanna, Ba'al, Artemis, and Zeus.

But scientists have done much more than just discover lost cities and study long-forgotten gods. **Scientists have given us humans the powers that ancient gods supposedly possessed—and even more.** In ancient stories, gods like Artemis and Zeus could see and hear things that happened on the other side of the world, and they could fly through the air. Now, because of science, any kid with a smartphone can easily see and hear things that happen on the other side of the world. And thanks to science, you can also fly through the air in helicopters, airplanes, and spaceships, as if you were Artemis or Zeus.

In ancient stories Zeus could kill people from a distance with his thunderbolts and Artemis could pick off victims one by one with her magic arrows. Science has given even worse destructive powers to human presidents and generals. They can now kill millions of people all at once using missiles and nuclear bombs far stronger than any arrow or thunderbolt.

Science, of course, gave humans the power to heal as well as destroy. The gods in ancient stories could cure people of disease. Now science has given this ability to human doctors and inventors. When people are sick, they no longer go to the temples of Artemis and Zeus to beg these gods for a cure. Instead, they go to hospitals, where human doctors cure them with the help of medicines invented by human scientists.

Ancient stories also said that Zeus and Artemis could create animals and humans. Science is now giving some people the ability to create not only animals and humans but completely new kinds of creatures that no ancient mythology even imagined, like artificial intelligences (AIs).

But what exactly is science, and where did it come from? How is it different from all the stories people told about gods and dragons? And how can science help us solve the problems of famine, disease, and war?

Well, that's a whole different story.

Cahokia

Tenochtitlan

Tikal

Timbuktu

Cusco

Rapa Nui

WORLD MAP OF
HISTORY

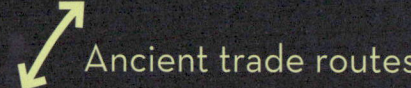 Ancient trade routes

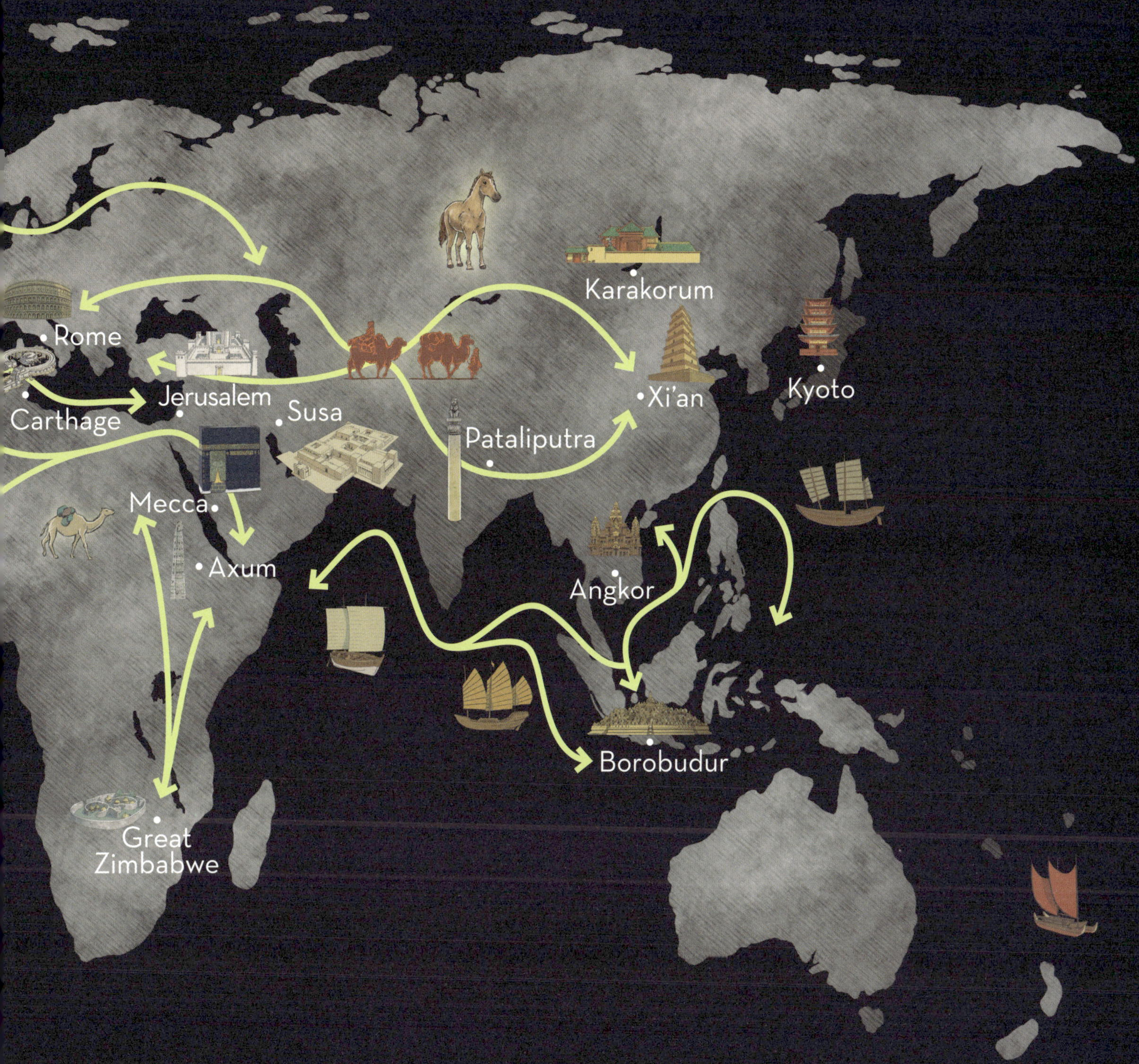

Karakorum
Rome
Carthage
Jerusalem
Susa
Xi'an
Kyoto
Pataliputra
Mecca
Axum
Angkor
Borobudur
Great Zimbabwe

ACKNOWLEDGMENTS

When you eat a fig or an orange, you have an entire tree to thank for it. Numerous leaves gathered the sunshine and numerous roots sucked the water that together formed a fruit. It is the same when you read a book—you have an entire team to thank for making it happen. Like every book, *Unstoppable Us* was created by many people working together. From fact-checkers to editors to translators, all their contributions are vital.

Special gratitude goes to the talented Ricard Zaplana Ruiz for his marvelous illustrations, to Jonathan Beck for championing the project, and to the experienced and inspiring Susanne Stark and Sebastian Ullrich for their invaluable advice and insights. The Sapienship team, led by the wonderful Naama Avital, not only initiated this delightful project but also played a central role in writing, editing, designing, researching, and global marketing this illustrated book series for young readers (of all ages!). The capable and creative Sapienship team includes: Naama Wartenburg, Ariel Retik, Hanna Shapiro, Jason Parry, Shay Abel, Daniel Taylor, Michael Zur, Jim Clarke, Dor Shilton,

Ray Brandon, Guangyu Chen, Nadav Neuman, Galiete Katzir, Dima Basov, Gilad Atlacevitz, Ayala Sorotsky, Anna Gontar, and Chen Avraham. Additional thanks to Friederike Fleschenberg, Adriana Hunter, and Adi Moreno, each of whom contributed significantly, and to Carolina Lopez-Ruiz and Anthony Kaldellis for their help.

My thanks also extend to all the translators who make this book available to so many people in so many languages.

Lastly, I am grateful for the love and encouragement from my mother Pnina, my sisters Einat and Liat, my nieces and nephews Tomer, Noga, Matan, Romi and Uri, and my husband Itzik, whose unwavering support made this book possible.

—YUVAL NOAH HARARI

Thanks to Iván Vázquez and Nigio for their advice on color. Dedicated to Dominique Campete, Irene Cordón, Mireia Serra, and the "Nata gratis" gang.

To all fellow Homo sapiens who share my profession, thank you for your knowledge and friendship.

To the team of professionals who make up Sapienship, thank you for your help and guidance through all the steps of the creative process.

And of course, to Yuval Noah Harari for trusting my illustrations and letting them travel halfway around the world with his text.

—RICARD ZAPLANA RUIZ

BOOKS BY YUVAL NOAH HARARI

Unstoppable Us, Volume 1:
How Humans Took Over the World

Unstoppable Us, Volume 2:
Why the World Isn't Fair

Sapiens: A Brief History of Humankind

Homo Deus: A Brief History of Tomorrow

21 Lessons for the 21st Century

Nexus: A Brief History of Information Networks from the Stone Age to AI

YUVAL NOAH HARARI is a historian, philosopher, and the bestselling author of *Sapiens: A Brief History of Humankind*, *Homo Deus: A Brief History of Tomorrow*, *21 Lessons for the 21st Century*, and *Sapiens: A Graphic History*. His books have sold 45 million copies in 65 languages, and he is considered one of the world's most influential public intellectuals today. Born in Israel in 1976, Harari received his PhD from the University of Oxford in 2002 and is currently a lecturer at the Department of History in the Hebrew University of Jerusalem. He is a distinguished research fellow at the University of Cambridge's Centre for the Study of Existential Risk. In 2019, Harari co-founded Sapienship with his husband, Itzik Yahav. Sapienship is a social impact company with projects in the fields of entertainment and education, whose main goal is to focus the public conversation on the most important global challenges facing the world today.